THE QUESTION
OF GOVERNMENT

THE QUESTION
OF GOVERNMENT

An Inquiry Into the Breakdown
of Modern Political Systems

DAVID FROMKIN

CHARLES SCRIBNER'S SONS
NEW YORK

071818

Library of Congress Cataloging in Publication Data
Fromkin, David.
    The question of government.
        1. State, The.   I. Title.
JC251.F76   320'.2   74-13901
ISBN 0-684-13845-X

1 3 5 7 9 11 13 15 17 19   c/c   20 18 16 14 12 10 8 6 4 2

CONTENTS

1

AN ASSESSMENT OF GOVERNMENT

2

A ROMAN ROAD

3

DEFINING THE FUNCTION OF GOVERNMENT

4

THE LIMITS OF GOVERNMENT

5

THE SEARCH FOR AN ALTERNATIVE TO GOVERNMENT

6

OUT FROM EDEN

NOTES

INDEX

PREFACE

The concepts outlined in the following pages were conceived and developed over the course of many eventful years. The general theory of politics proposed in chapter six was my comment on an unpublished manuscript by Dr. F. Palmer Weber in 1962, the year of the Cuban missile episode. The international law chapter derives from a paper I delivered to The Center for the Study of Democratic Institutions in 1965, the year that President Johnson embarked on his Vietnam war policy. Although this book was long since finished—indeed it was already being typeset—in the summer of 1974, when Richard Nixon resigned as President of the United States, the drama that preceded and precipitated the resignation dominated the newspaper headlines as I wrote and edited it.

It was tempting to comment on these and other current events as they occurred, advocating specific policies, because the basic principles of government and politics that I have tried to elucidate underlie my view of particular situations. But it seemed unwise to do so, for it would have distracted attention from the primary concerns of a work that necessarily ranges over long periods of time. In the following pages I have attempted to develop a theory about the role of government in human history and about the crisis in that historical role caused by the scientific and industrial revolutions of the last few centuries. If such an endeavor is to be accomplished, it can only be by advancing a general political philosophy rather than a specific political program; and so that is what I have tried to do.

New York City
August 27, 1974

THE QUESTION
OF GOVERNMENT

1

AN ASSESSMENT
OF GOVERNMENT

In the ordinary course of events, the assumptions upon
which people base their lives are taken for granted; they
go unexamined, like faces that blur into a crowd. To an
increasing extent, however, a recognition of them is
forced upon us by the exigencies of our time. Circumstances compel it because events seem no longer to flow
in an ordinary course. A thousand years ago nobody gave
much thought to the air that envelops the earth. Today
we think about it all the time—not because of any rise in
the general level of consciousness, but because it has
become questionable whether it is healthy for us to
breathe it. What is true of the physical atmosphere is also
true of the intellectual one: only when the most fundamental views are questioned do we fully realize that we
do in fact hold them and that they may require careful
scrutiny; otherwise they fade into the landscape of
existence, unnoticed.

It therefore suggests an uneasiness about modern
society when a major American university, the Massachusetts Institute of Technology, offers a course of study

in a new academic discipline called institutional assessment, which proposes a critical evaluation, not merely of
one, but of all the basic institutions of society, including
the university, the church, and the state. A clue to what
prompted so sweeping a program is provided by the
subject of the course during the 1973–74 academic year:
the failure of human systems.

The political government of society should be among
the institutions most intensively studied. No institution is
more pervasive. None is a greater failure at the present
time. If a lack of success is the precondition for reassessment, then no institution is more in need of reassessment
than that of government. A recent survey of public
opinion in the United States showed that 66 percent of
the population is dissatisfied with the way in which the
country is being governed. Much of this dissatisfaction
can be ascribed to the Watergate-related scandals of the
Nixon administration; but it really goes far beyond the
moral vagaries of any one administration to a more
general feeling, a feeling shared by the peoples of many
other countries—a general sense of distrust of their
governments and disappointment in their achievements.

Where and why and to what extent have governments
failed? What can be done about it? What actually is the
nature and function of government as such? What are its
limitations and its potential? Obviously this is not the
first time in history that such questions have been posed;
they have been asked before, especially in times of
political crisis and uncertainty. Moreover, they have
been answered, although not always in ways that seem
relevant or helpful today. The answers provided by the

ancient and modern literature in the field of governmental science have been various and contradictory, but share a common failing: they emerge from a limited perspective that does not entirely accommodate itself to the differing patterns of societies other than their own. We need a longer perspective than they provide; we need one long enough to transcend parochial boundaries. It is true that the words we use to describe the concept of government are rooted in the language of our own classics; but the institution of government has roots that grow far deeper, and a proper perception of it must be proportioned, not to the word, but to the thing.

The English word for government derives from the Latin *gubernare* and the Greek (transliterated as) *kybernaien,* both of which meant "to steer (a ship)." The institution, however, in its dual aspect of giving direction and of those who give the direction is far older than Greeks and Romans. Indeed, it seems to be as old as the human race. Its elements of dominance, leadership, and hierarchy are (ethologists claim) among the distinguishing characteristics of primates; and Jane Goodall has observed them in our closest cousins, the chimpanzees. At some unknown point these characteristics crystallized in a regular and continuous way and became government.

Government is, if defined broadly enough, the basic and essential institution of human society. It must exist whenever and wherever human society is or has been found, for, as Austin Ranney has observed, "there is no recorded instance of an actual society, past or present, that has operated for long with no government whatsoever." It pervades all the history and actuality of humanity; and that is why it is so curious that its study has been parochial. Government is not restricted to one time or place; but, in contrast, its students have been severely constrained by the limitations imposed by their own time and place. Aristotle, first and greatest of its scholars,* lived in what we have come to call a city-state; and so he studied government by analyzing the constitutions of city-states. It has always been thus: each generation studies government by examining the governments with which it is familiar. So shall it be, even with you and me; we are all of us prisoners of time and bear the mark of its shackles upon ourselves and upon our works. Ignoring or forgetting this is the most human and understandable of errors, and one that we all seem to commit at one time or another: thinking that we are everyone, and that the place in which we live is everywhere, and that the time in which we live is always and forever. But it is an error that distorts with especial violence the study of an institution that does in fact deal with everyone and with everywhere for as always and forever as the lifetime of human society itself.

The error, of course, is not in seeing through our own eyes; the error lies in forgetting that it *is* only through our own eyes that we see. The data of which we are aware is limited, thus partial. Our perception of the data is personal; thus, at worst it is flawed or mistaken, and at

---

* It is true that Plato and others thought about and taught about government; but Aristotle was the first whom we know to have systematically studied it.

best it represents only one of a number of valid points of view. The concepts we employ to organize these perceptions are themselves prejudicial. There is no completely satisfactory way to overcome these weaknesses, but an awareness of them can help to limit the distortions they introduce. Indeed, an understanding of them might enable us to make them work for us rather than against us; thus the architect of the Parthenon made its lines curved so that they would appear to be straight.

It is odd that an awareness of the significance of the angle-of-vision has been so late in coming to political science. An appreciation of its significance has characterized the other sciences since the very earliest days of civilization, even before the Phoenician flotilla in Pharaoh's service circumnavigated Africa and found that the heavens looked different when viewed from the southern hemisphere. It has characterized fiction as well as fact. In literature, wrote Somerset Maugham, ". . . the *I* who writes is just as much a character in the story as the other persons with whom it is concerned." Henry James, in the Preface to *The Golden Bowl*, asserted that when he wrote a novel, he wrote it ". . . not as my own impersonal account of the affairs in hand, but as my account of somebody's impression of it."

Only in recent years, however, has political science begun to arrive at this same state of understanding. The study of international relations has taken the lead in this regard, with its focus on the problems of perception and misperception in the dealings between different nations. It is a lead that ought to be followed. Governmental science, too, needs to be placed in historical perspective if it is to be seen aright.

The necessity for doing so is all the greater at the present time because we wrongly continue to view events in this area from a vantage point that in other respects we have abandoned and left behind. The concept of government still taught in the United States derives from a period in the country's past that is recent in terms of chronological years but far distant in terms of outlook and experience. It was a period in which America rose to glory and triumph, overcame the Great Depression, rescued the world from darkness by winning the two greatest wars in history, and finally (as we then thought) emerged as the wealthiest and most powerful nation on earth. The outlook of America at that time was born of success: of problems solved, of difficulties overcome, and of victories gained. In a characteristic phrase of the 1940s, it was said that having won the war, we would now "win the peace." Americans at that time were confident of their ability to secure peace and prosperity; they had learned their lessons from the errors of the 1930s, and felt they knew the governmental techniques that would bring full employment at home and collective security abroad. The prevailing mood was one of satisfaction with ourselves, with our national ideals, with our institutions and their capacity for adaptation and growth, and with our future. In the intoxication of V-Day it seemed that for Americans history moved in only one direction: up. The United States emerged from the Second World War an open, unafraid nation, united in purpose and sure of itself. Americans agreed with

Europeans who said we were innocent—perhaps not quite so innocent as in the novels of Henry James (had we been, ever?), but innocent still; yet we knew it was that very quality that had enabled us to draw the sword from the stone. As outsiders bitterly observed, we were a nation without a sense of tragedy; there were no lines under our eyes, no furrows on our brow, no marks on our body, no scars on our soul.

It was at that high point of enthusiasm and optimism that the contemporary American concept of government took authoritative form in the book in which Charles E. Merriam, the dean of American political scientists, summed up his lifetime of knowledge and wisdom. Merriam was a commanding and seminal figure in the study of governmental sciences in America. For thirty years he was the head of the department of political science at the University of Chicago. He and his brilliant pupil, Harold Lasswell, taught or influenced the leading figures who still dominate academic political science in America today—David Easton, Gabriel A. Almond, David E. Apter, and the other luminaries of the so-called Chicago school.

In *Systematic Politics* (1945), Merriam attempted his most ambitious academic undertaking. He sought to do what many believe had never been adequately done before, and what some believe had never really been done before at all: he attempted, within the confines of a single work, to write a systematic description and discussion of the institution of government—not the government of one or more nations, but government as such, government in general, government in all its aspects and varieties. The work was greatly praised, and with good reason. It accomplished many of its author's objectives. Yet it failed to guard sufficiently against the misperceptions current in the year in which it was written; and indeed, it reflected the excessive enthusiasms of that year to a fault. It is a book that is vintage 1945: it tastes of victory and knows no insoluble problems. It concedes that there are, and will be, difficulties, but is confident that they will be overcome. It admits that there are answers we do not know at the present time, but asserts that in the future—probably soon—we will find them, for new disciplines afford us broad perspectives unavailable to the men and women of prior times. It supposes that with wider awareness we are in the process of achieving a deeper understanding of human nature and human society, and that we are also moving towards perfecting government itself.

Merriam saw the whole life process as a creative evolution in which the values of the human species continually rise. The process was seen as a transition from darkness to light, from slavery to freedom; an imperfect yesterday had led to a good today, which would lead to a better tomorrow. At the heart of *Systematic Politics*, and animating the whole of that work, is an abiding faith in the capacity of government to satisfy the growing range of human and social needs:

Government is the oldest and in some ways the best-tried agency of mankind, and, whatever its temporary aberrations may be—and they are many—there is no reason to conclude that government cannot be kept abreast of the advancing waves of human progress. *Its principles and its techniques are capable of dealing with any human problem* if they are co-ordinated and inspired by public support and confidence, by faith as well as by force, by intelligence as well as by passion. (*italics added*)

When read literally, the words beginning with "if" seem to be reneging on the courageous assertions that have gone before; but given the optimistic spirit of the work, no real qualification seems to have been intended to the expression of profound confidence and belief.

It is interesting that a basic condition of Merriam's faith was not clearly alluded to in the sentences quoted above. It relates to the particular type of government to which he referred. It was only in democratic government that Merriam had faith. Perhaps he did not think to stress it because it seemed that the cause was won. "The modern long-time trend is in the direction of democracy," he wrote, and in 1945 the issue seemed to have been settled.

Merriam's views in *Systematic Politics* are worth discussing at this length for their own sake, because they constitute a milestone intellectual view of the role of government in world history. What is of even greater significance here, however, is the impact they have had on American life and thought. They permeate the attitudes of Merriam's pupils, who are our teachers. They inform the inflated expectations that have led to one public disappointment after another. And, perhaps most important, they constitute a prevailing American doctrine of government that is at variance even with the facts of life as we ourselves have experienced and perceived them. The discrepancy between our philosophical attitude toward government and the way in which we experience governmental reality is one of the reasons for the current widespread disillusionment with the political process.

Merriam attempted, with brilliance, erudition, and skill, to take a general, overall view. He was aware that details of his description of the political process would have to be modified in the light of future data, but he was clearly unaware that his organizing concepts were merely "a point of view"—and a somewhat out-of-date one at that. Tested against the experience of contemporary politics, as variously perceived in overlapping views, Merriam's satisfaction with our own form of government seems complacent and his confidence in its inevitable triumph seems unduly optimistic. His study of government was an uncritical affirmation of faith; ours must be a critical assessment. That is what we should have learned since 1945—if not before. Idealism is an American vice as well as an American virtue. Skepticism is something we have had to import from abroad. Indeed, it is largely due to a number of brilliant scholars who were born in Europe that a measure of realism and balance have been brought into the American appraisal of global affairs. This was all the more necessary because world events since 1945 have been so out of harmony with our previous enthusiastic expectations.

The Cold War, to begin with, challenged all sorts of beliefs that Merriam and, indeed, the American public as a whole, took for granted. It was for this reason that the United States was so shocked and confused by the onset of its confrontation with the Soviet Union. Americans at the time (and many even now) could not understand how, in the moment that American democracy had won global triumph, the nation's security and the cause of freedom had suddenly come to be in mortal jeopardy. Had the victory been betrayed? Had it been squandered in unthinking wastefulness? Where had it gone?

The most intellectually influential answer to these questions was that given by George Kennan in a series of lectures published in 1951. In his response he too spoke to the problem of angle-of-vision awareness and the hazards of misperception. Kennan claimed that we had deluded ourselves in many ways, among them that we had never won the great war for democracy that we thought we had won. It was not that winged victory had somehow flown away; it was that the fickle goddess had never been there in the first place—she had come only in our dreams, not in our waking reality.

Kennan began his analysis of American delusions by describing them as they existed at the turn of the century, at a time when people in this country felt a sense of national security such as no people had felt for a very long time—perhaps not since the flowering of the early Roman Empire in the age of the Antonines. The security was real, but its cause was misunderstood. Its cause was thought to be America's superior wisdom and virtue; but its real cause, as we can see now, was the position of Great Britain, shielding us from the Continent—a position which in turn depended on a balance of power such that no single nation could dominate the entire Eurasian mass. It was because of this misunderstanding, according to Kennan, that after paying the immense price of two world wars, which we ostensibly won, we ended up with much less security and a much less satisfactory international situation than when we began.

Had we understood that the condition of our security was the balance of continental power, we would have entered the First World War in order to preserve that balance, and we would have conducted and concluded the war in such a fashion as to restore the balance. In fact, we did quite the contrary. Once we were drawn into the war, we deluded ourselves into thinking we were fighting for righteous causes, primarily the punishment of Germany for having forced us into a fight we did not want. Had we been fighting to restore the balance, as Kennan argues we should have been doing, we would have pursued as our chief strategic goal the shortening of the war, so as to preserve the energies, the equilibrium, and the stability of Europe. Presumably this would have meant a negotiated settlement of an indecisive war; but we, on the contrary, crusaded against Germany in an effort to defeat her so crushingly that she would never force us to fight her again. The result of our crusade was the collapse of the old order in Europe, untold turmoil, and the rise of fascism, nazism, and communism. We had let the genie out of the bottle; and by the 1930s the demonic forces controlled a preponderance of power in the world.

In 1939, according to Kennan, although it may not have been perceived by government leaders in the United States and western Europe, the balance of world power had turned decisively against us. We would have had no hope of defeating a combination of Nazi Germany, Soviet Russia, and imperial Japan, all of them entities deeply and dangerously hostile to western democracy. The war could not be won. Our only chance was to form an alliance with one of the hostile powers against the other two, hoping for a partial victory; and then, having eliminated two out of three, we could turn to oppose on more equal terms the remaining hostile power, which had briefly, temporarily, and perhaps uneasily, been our ally. It is a course that we happened to follow, without actually intending to or even knowing it.

Because we continued to delude ourselves about what we were doing, we were quite surprised to find ourselves in a Cold War. We were not the sort of people to matter-of-factly ally ourselves with a tyranny like Stalin's, so we had to pretend, even to ourselves, that the Soviet Union was a friend to democracy. This meant that the 1945 victory was conceived of as a global victory for the free world; and thus we were shocked to find half the world still in chains and controlled by forces hostile to our ideals and to our interests. We had only achieved a partition of the world; and partition—as we were also to see in India, in Palestine, and in Ireland—was not necessarily a solution that the involved parties could regard as final.

The Soviet Union may have been as surprised as we were by the Cold War, although for opposite reasons. There is no reason to suppose that the Soviet leaders ever deluded themselves, as ours did, about the nature of the alliance. They seem to have been fully aware of the fact that it was one of convenience, designed to secure mutual interest and advantage. Their armies had driven the

Germans from eastern and central Europe to meet the western armies halfway across the Continent. There was now a frontier; but instead of sharing on the basis of that dividing line, the American government pressed for the restoration of national independence and the institution of democracy in eastern Europe. We were keeping our half, but did not want them to keep theirs. This must have made us seem a greedy and unprincipled partner, seeking to take advantage of an unexpectedly favorable situation (our discovery of the atom bomb) to pocket all the winnings. Our government was not insincere, it was merely unrealistic; but the Soviets probably were too gullible to believe that. They could not have been expected to believe that the American leaders had been so fatuously self-deluded throughout the war about the goals for which the war was being fought. Never were two governments so ill-equipped to understand one another. The Soviet leaders were honest with themselves and dishonest only in their dealings with others; our leaders were just the reverse.

So we lurched, without any real comprehension of what was happening, into global conflict; and George Kennan's explanation of how we got there kicks the props out from under Merriam's excessively optimistic view of democratic government. Merriam saw democracy forging ahead and bound to win. Kennan showed democracy coming from behind, drawing even, and then entering a contest of uncertain outcome.

It is not intended to suggest that George Kennan's views were or are universally accepted. On the contrary, there have been reconsiderations, revisions, and historical explanations of different and contrary sorts; none of them, however, validates the Merriam concept, and in that one respect all are in accord with Kennan. Revisionist historians, for example, take a far less flattering view of the motivations of the American government; and this critical view can be construed to mean that they challenge the belief that unique virtue resides in our system of democratic government. They challenge Merriam in one way; the followers of Kennan challenge him in another. The common ground of attack is that the views represented by *Systematic Politics* did not adequately prepare us for what happened after 1945.

The realities of the Cold War involved a drastic scaling down of what could be expected from governmental action. Our adversaries would not follow our lead; and, unilaterally, we could not achieve all the desirable results we had hoped for. The Soviet Union thwarted many of our most constructive initiatives. They did not participate in our international monetary institutions or in our international development programs. They refused to participate in the Marshall Plan for the reconstruction of Europe. As we saw it, and as we looked on helplessly, they lowered an iron curtain across the Continent and raised a wall across divided Berlin. Heirs to Byzantium, they revived the Eastern Empire, and under the banner of progress plunged back centuries in time to reimpose the division of Europe into East and West, which had been the work of the Caesars.

For more than a quarter of a century, American armies have been stationed along the periphery of the Communist world, like legionnaires on the Roman frontier or Chinese at the Great Wall standing guard against the barbarians. During much of that time it has appeared that the most effective limitation on the power of our government to go forward and create a peaceful, free, and prosperous world order was the power of the Soviet bloc, which seemed to us to be committed to a contrary design. Political theorists during the years of the Cold War tended therefore to emphasize a distinction (which for Merriam had been unnecessary) between democratic government on the one hand and Communist totalitarian government on the other. Where Merriam had seen the concept of government as a unity, it was now seen as a dichotomy. Furthermore, the cause of free government was not seen as necessarily in the ascendant. Indeed, a 1972 study concluded that two-thirds of the world's people lived in countries that were not free. We were far from *Systematic Politics*, far from the end of the Second World War, and certainly far from realizing the high hopes that emerged from that great victory.

If the cause of government depends on the prospects for enlarging the area in which free institutions flourish, then its chances were at that time uncertain. Some saw the battle between the free world and its enemies as unlikely to be resolved in a satisfactory fashion. Others saw it as unlikely to be resolved at all; indeed, there were those who saw the Cold War conflict as more-or-less permanent, if not eternal. They perceived the dichotomy of government in a vast historical framework in which the threat posed by the Soviet Union was viewed as being merely the current episode in a much longer drama, the purported historical conflict between Asia and Europe, between East and West, which was postulated (with a diverting mythical explanation) in the first known work of prose literature, the historical narrative of Herodotus, written in the fifth century B.C.

The East-West dichotomy has been important to the thought and work of diverse and important authors throughout the years; and yet there is a very persuasive case to be made for the proposition that "Asia" is a meaningless term when used in a nongeographical sense, because the major cultures that have flourished in the East have been essentially diverse rather than unified. This point of view, of course, makes the dichotomy quite meaningless.

The concept of "the West," too, is not without ambiguity. If by it we mean the free and open society described in Pericles' "Funeral Oration," which for 2,500 years has articulated the political ideals of what we call the West, then most of Europe must be excluded for most of its history. If by it we mean a society that has its foundations in Greco-Roman culture and the Christian religion, then the vast numbers of our citizens who have not read the classics and are not practicing Christians have excluded themselves from it. If by it we mean Europe and the countries colonized by Europeans, there are still difficulties: Spain has not always seen herself as part of Europe; and if Turgenev was seen as distinctly European, it is precisely because many other Russians were not. Australia and New Zealand are Western only if you defy geography. Charles de Gaulle, whose Atlantic-to-the-Urals conception embodied a rigorous insistence on geography, embraced within his definition European

Russia (the oriental despots, who were supposedly our foes), while excluding the United States (we who, under Truman, Eisenhower, and Kennedy, thought that *we were* the West). The Japanese are now considered a Western and, indeed, an Atlantic power, because they are an advanced industrial society and an ally—which makes political and economic sense, but geographical nonsense.

As an operative term in describing the political configuration of the post-1945 world, "the West" is increasingly open to both practical and theoretical objections. For the last fifteen years the French government has made a particular point of denying the validity of the concept. It has pursued a policy of going its own way, putting what it sees as national interests ahead of so-called Western interests, which it regards as a euphemism for American interests. And without France, it is less easy to think of the alliance in any complete sense as embodying "the West." Indeed, the concept of government as being distinctly either Eastern or Western in character is increasingly both questionable and questioned. In this one respect, the difference between our institutions and those of our adversaries is not woven into the fabric of existence. The allegedly eternal conflict between East and West is an illusion. Differences do exist between the nations, but they are of another sort.

The consequences of the American foreign policy currently pursued by Henry Kissinger provide an example of this. Despite the liquidation of many Cold War issues, the relaxation of tensions previously characterizing relations between the two nations, and the development of cooperative approaches to the solution of some of the world's problems that carry a high risk of military confrontation, the Soviet Union and the United States are not able at the present time to cooperate in a sufficient number of positive and constructive programs for the building of a better world. They cannot do so because they do not share a common view of what constitutes a better world. The end of the Cold War has not brought with it an increase in the power of American democracy to realize its ideals on a global scale, such as we thought had been achieved in 1945. Indeed, the international conference of oil-consuming states in February 1974 underscored once more in dramatic fashion the fact that even nations believed to be our allies and those believed to have interests identical to our own do not perceive their interests and loyalties in the same way that we perceive them; nor do they share, necessarily, American ideas of how the world should be organized. The power of the government of the United States to affect the world's circumstances remains limited, even though Cold War differences have been somewhat resolved and even though the difference between East and West never actually existed.

For Thomas Mann, who saw deeply into the life of our and other times, a personal and also more meaningful geographical dichotomy than the East-West one was provided by the distinction between North and South, which afforded real differences in culture and temperament. This was E. M. Forster's theme, too, and that of Norman Douglas in his joyous moral fable, *South Wind*.

The difference between the industrial North and the

agricultural South is basic. Novelists have long emphasized it, but for some reason political scientists have not.
We Americans, descendants of Grant and Sherman, Lee
and Stonewall Jackson, Lincoln and Douglas, Davis and
Benjamin—we, who collectively have spent hundreds of
millions of hours contemplating Scarlett O'Hara and her
adventurous career—should see with especial clarity, by
extending our experience, that the Mason-Dixon line
runs around the world.

The North-South line of division, despite contrary
assertions, is not a racial one. The substitution of race for
class as the agency of revolutionary action is an imbecil-
ity that the Left has now borrowed from the Right; but
the concept has not acquired any validity in the process
of transfer. The line of division is actually industrialization and not pigmentation. It has to do with the color of
your money, not with the color of your skin.

Needs, conditions, and cultures are somewhat different
in the southern countries; but these distinctions were
ignored by American government, business, and academic figures, whose theory was in the Merriam tradition. The theory was that these countries should adopt
American institutions of government; and that, if they
did so, they would be able to achieve the industrial and
economic goals they had set for themselves. What, then,
was the explanation for the failure of southern governments to modernize and industrialize their countries after
the Second World War, despite the help and advice we
gave them? Why did they install military dictatorships in
place of democratic governments if, as we claimed, only
democracy could supply a country with what it needed?

Once again, our 1945 view of the world was contradicted by contemporary experiences. As an export model, our institutions of government were not a success. They seemed not to be so universally valid as Merriam and others had thought that they were.

North or South, East or West, all differences and conflicts have come to be overshadowed by the nuclear peril. It, too—or it above all, as some would say—cast doubt upon the efficacy of the existing types of government. At about the same time that Merriam was writing *Systematic Politics*, and on the same campus, physicists unleashed a new force that could destroy the world that Merriam wrote of governing. In a squash court under the west stands of Stagg Field, the sustained nuclear chain reaction took place that made possible the atomic bomb. As almost everybody said that they realized, an altogether novel situation had been created by the invention of such a demonic tool. In the past, conflicts that could not be settled in some other way had always been resolved on the battlefield; but the new weapon made it too dangerous to go on doing so. Scientists who had calculated the potential destructiveness of the bomb seriously warned that mankind would be destroyed if there were another world war. Permanent peace, which had always been a dream, now appeared to have become an immediate necessity. This seemed to mean that a world government was necessary and that it alone would be capable of preventing national governments from engaging in warfare. Robert Hutchins, chancellor of the University of Chicago, took the lead in the writing of a proposed constitution for the future world government.

For purposes of the present discussion the important point about the world-government group was the feature they identified as the fundamental weakness of government when faced with the atomic threat: it was, they said, too small. No emphasis was given in this context to the distinction between the capabilities of one kind of national government and those of another kind; for them the overriding distinction was between national government of any kind on the one hand and supranational government on the other. Only the latter, it was felt, was likely to prove capable of saving the human race from suicidal warfare.

Academics and idealists were joined to some extent by government officials in recognizing the splitting of the atom as a unique event, radically altering the situation of world society and requiring new dispositions. The Baruch-Acheson-Lilienthal plan advanced by the United States after the Second World War defined the minimum requirements of this point of view. It proposed the creation of a world authority that would monopolize the development and control of atomic energy. In effect, the plan suggested the creation of a world government, the sole and exclusive purpose of which would be to govern the production and use of atomic energy. This reflected the view that national governments had become inadequate in only one respect: that they were unable to deal with the military ramifications of atomic power.

The years should have strengthened the arguments in favor of a supranational solution. New developments have made it conceivable that cheap and easily-made nuclear weapons will soon be within the manufacturing capability of dozens of countries, and that such weapons therefore may become available to all manner of groups and individuals, including the fanatic and the deranged. If anything, the answer seems more clear and urgent than it did in 1945. Although it also has become commonplace to assert it, in the long run nothing smaller than a government for the human species as it exists on this earth will prove satisfactory. Until recently only the madcap visionary Left spoke in terms of the Parliament of Mankind; now even so unmadcap an institution as the Roman Catholic church does so, at least to the extent that its views are reflected by the encyclical *Pacem in Terris*, in which Pope John XXIII called for "fundamental changes in the political structure of the world," and wrote that:

. . . Today the universal common good poses problems of world-wide dimensions, which cannot be adequately tackled or solved except by the efforts of public authorities endowed with a wideness of powers, structure and means of the same proportions: that is, of public authorities which are in a position to operate in an effective manner on a world-wide basis. The moral order itself, therefore, demands that such a form of public authority be established.

A currently prevailing view, however, holds that the nuclear danger has been exaggerated. The wars we and others have fought since 1945, without recourse to the ultimate weapon, are supposed to have shown that in actual practice governments do recognize and understand that nuclear weapons are unusable. But they may not always do so. The fact that the weapons have not been used in these wars does not guarantee that they will

not be used in the future. The danger has not material-
ized, but neither has it disappeared.

In part, the danger persists because the relevant
governments have not attempted to defend against it.
Some scientists claim that protective systems are feasible;
others disagree. At the moment the question is no more
than theoretical. Whether or not national governments
can protect their populations from the consequences of
nuclear warfare has become a merely academic issue, for
the governments of the major powers have not tried to do
so. Our own government has adopted a nuclear strategy
that assumes the United States would be destroyed at the
outset of a nuclear war against the Soviet Union. Our
strategy (which suffers the acronym MAD—Mutual
Assured Destruction) consists in the maintenance of a
weaponry system that, were we devastated by a nuclear
attack, would destroy the Soviet Union in return. Our
computers would avenge us, for nobody else would be left
to do so. It is less a defense policy than a suicide pact.

There is, it must be said, a considerable amount of
method in the MADness. It has a crazy logic of its own,
though it is not one with which it is possible to be much
at ease. The rationale of MAD is prevention or, in the
usual word, deterrence: if each government can be
persuaded that destroying the other country would
necessarily result in destroying its own, neither side will
attack. It is crucial, though, that neither side be allowed
mistakenly to believe itself attacked, for it would then
embark on a retaliative attack, and that would be the
end of both. To reassure one another, each side deliber-

ately leaves itself vulnerable. Neither side attempts any genuine nuclear-defense program against the other.* Defensive measures might be misinterpreted—activities along this line might seem to indicate a plan to protect against retaliation, thus implying an intent to attack. For the moment neither side can destroy the offensive capability of the other, although some may say that technologically this will soon no longer be true; but it is essential to MAD that it remain true.

MAD assumes that both powers will play by the same rules, which implies that the rules are understood in the same way by both. This may not be the case. For example, the United States apparently believes that both sides would stop at a reciprocal low (or "tactical") level of nuclear warfare; the Soviet Union, according to a widely respected study, does not. Indeed, there is disagreement as to what constitutes, for purposes of retaliation or deterrence, a nuclear weapon. MAD also assumes continuous rationality and accurate perception at the top level of national decision making, for if one government attacks through mistake or through fanatical folly, it is the end of us all. MAD, in other words, must work 100 percent of the time; and it is this defect that has provoked some of its opponents' most persuasive arguments. Our government's policy is inadequate because it copes only with the dangers that might arise from rational behavior and predictable events. If ours were a truly effective

* Some limited programs are permitted by mutual agreement, and smaller programs may perhaps be undertaken that would prove effective only against a third power.

policy, it would also guard against the irrational and the accidental. Its excuse for not doing so is that the world has been so transformed by modern science that it is no longer possible to do so.

It amounts to a confession that the political structure of the country (and, by extension, of *every* country) has become at least partially obsolete. The government of the United States was established by the Constitution in part "to provide for the common defense." The projected military budget for the fiscal year commencing July 1, 1974, was $85.8 billion; but for all the enormous expenditure, the government deliberately made no provisions for the defense of the United States against Soviet nuclear attack. The armed forces of the United States exist in their present form and on their present scale largely in order to prevent the outbreak of a war that, should it occur, they intend neither to wage, nor to win—that, indeed, they have the competence neither to wage nor to win. The government of what is often called the most powerful nation in history is unable to do what any chimpanzee leader or pygmy chief can do in terms of his own world. To that extent, the constitutional responsibility to provide for the common defense went up in smoke at Hiroshima.

It would be different if MAD were an unreasonable national strategy. Then it would be simply a policy that should be overturned. As it is, its burlesque quality, which makes it seem a caricature of rationalism gone insane, derives from the altered circumstances of the political world to which it is a valid and logical response. It demonstrates the inappropriateness of traditional political structures to deal with the traditional tasks of politics in the new context created by modern science and technology. Once the governments of national commonwealths were so formidable that they were likened to Leviathan. Now, helpless and out of their element, they seem like whales cast up on a beach by a storm at sea.

The American government's position, explicit in the Baruch-Acheson-Lilienthal plan and implicit in MAD, is that the development of nuclear energy is the unique area in which national government has become inadequate. Circumstances have shown, however, that there are other areas of inadequacy. A case in point is the inability of industrial nations, at least up until now, to cope with the growth of multinational corporations. These corporations are believed by some observers (and by some participants) to have enough power to undermine the control that the central banks of each nation have hitherto exercised over national currency. This is particularly threatening because control of monetary policy is central to the management of a modern industrial society and the achievement of social policy.

According to an authoritative study by the United States Tariff Commission, $268 billion of short-term liquid assets were held at the end of 1971 by private institutions participating in international finance. This vast amount was more than twice the total of all international reserves held by all central banks and international monetary institutions in the world at the same date. These figures have been contested by critics, but the question that they pose is inescapable. Has control over national economic destinies indeed passed from the cabinet room to the board room?

Like so many post-Second World War dangers, this one has been presented in a lurid light. The three hundred largest industrial corporations, we are told, already produce one-sixth of the earth's industrial output; they will produce one-half by the end of the century if they continue to grow at their present rate. Moreover, if a corporation's sales were to be equated with a nation's output of goods and services, then fifty-one of the world's one hundred biggest money powers would be international corporations and only forty-nine would be countries. In the spring of 1973 *The Wall Street Journal* suggested that the growth of the multinationals was "creating an economic and social movement that some observers compare in significance to the Industrial Revolution."

Thus national governments have lost some control over the levers of power that would enable them to deal with levels of employment, wages, prices, industrial development, agriculture, raw materials, and the other vital constituents of the economy. The governments have watched, seemingly helpless, confused, and divided, as the power over prosperity, growth, and stability has slipped from their hands. Indeed, the only immediate counterpoise to the multinational firms seems to be the growing power of multinational labor unions. What these unions want, according to their spokesmen, is a voice in planning and management: the power, once again, to affect and overshadow national economic policies.

The immediate disturbance blamed on the multinationals is the loss of control over international currencies. As with atomic energy, some have proposed solutions along the lines of the Baruch-Acheson-Lilienthal plan— that is, it has been suggested that a supranational agency of some sort be created to deal with this second and supposedly isolated instance in which national governments prove to be too small to handle a problem of this magnitude. For example, following Walter Bagehot, who proposed the first central bank for a modern nation, there are those who propose a central bank for the modern world. Evidence suggests, however, that there is little chance that national governments will unite in the foreseeable future to create a world agency to deal with any of these matters.

The unregulated power of the multinational corporations to affect the world economy was highlighted in another context by the oil panic of 1973–74. In the face of an asserted Arab embargo and of what was said to be a worldwide shortage of petroleum, decisions as to how the scarce resources should be shared between the various nations were made by the giant oil companies. The decision-making power came to them by default. National governments were powerless to make the decisions on an individual basis and were too divided to make the decisions on a cooperative basis.

The energy problem also cast into relief the whole question of finite and dwindling natural resources in a world consuming them at a growing rate. Somebody will have to plan ahead in order to develop alternative resources so that they will be available when needed. Somebody will have to plan to raise the investment capital necessary to realize such a program. These things have to be done for the world as a whole. Yet there is no government that can speak or act for the world as a whole.

The spectrum of governmental inadequacy is also widening considerably in the face of dangers to the human environment. In particular, these concern the seas and other international waterways, the pollution of which leads to the ruin of beaches and of the tourist trade, the destruction of oyster beds and fishing grounds, and the annihilation of entire species of sea life. All of these directly and seriously damage commercial interests; yet frequently the governments of the injured countries are helpless to act, for the acts of pollution often are committed beyond their frontiers, by other nations or by ships at sea. Nuclear tests conducted far away also lead to contamination by air and sea for which there is no redress, poisoning the future as well as the present by jeopardizing children, even those unborn and those unconceived.

The threatened death of the world ocean, which would be followed by the death of the world, is a matter beyond the competence of individual national governments. In the autumn of 1972, ninety-one nations concluded a convention to forbid the dumping of highly toxic substances into the open seas. It was a step forward, but a small one, for each nation was put on its honor to police itself, to penalize itself—and to excuse itself in case of emergency.

First steps, indeed, are being taken to lay the framework of international cooperative action. There was, for example, the Conference on the Human Environment convened by the United Nations in Stockholm in 1972. Bilateral talks between the United States and the Soviet Union have also proved productive. Unfortunately, the perceived interests of the governments that want to industrialize their nations without bearing the cost of pollution control, and of the other governments that want to protect their environments and their fishing and tourist industries from destructive pollution, remain adverse. Stalemate continues to be the rule, not the exception. And all the while perils mount and bizarre deaths are foreseen for the human race. Among them are the eventual possibility of smothering to death from smog; depletion of the earth's oxygen supply; and destruction of the ozone layer by supersonic commercial airplanes, so that life on earth, unprotected from ultraviolet radiation, would be destroyed. Scientists are pessimistic, too, about the traditional fight against drought and famine.

Overpopulation and its consequences remain a central concern. It has been claimed that dinosaurs died of overcrowding and that groups of mice were doomed to extinction through lack of sexual activity which followed once overpopulation destroyed their social organization and deformed their behavior. Elaborate and exotic analogies aside, the strain on world resources that would be caused by the foreseen growth in the world population in the next century would have catastrophic consequences jeopardizing the survival of our species or of any other.

One of the chief characteristics of our time is the

variety of terrible fates predicted for the human race. Are we taking it all too seriously? There have been times before when it was believed that the end of the world was at hand, and it did not happen. The curious sects that flourished during the English Civil War harbored strong fears of the impending End, scheduled for 1655–56. Astronomers had predicted that the end would come in 1365. At the approach of the year 1000, expectation of the end of the world was rampant; but in fact, the tenth century marked the beginning of such vital economic growth that present-day historians, looking back, cannot believe that the people initiating that growth could really have believed all the talk of death and doom. Do we, too, suffer from such unwarranted *fin-de-millénium* despair?

There are, of course, significant differences between now and then. The dangers we now face are not supernatural. They are palpable and measurable. They exist. They extend to the whole of life on the planet. It would not be like the catastrophes of yesteryear: the crumbling of ancient empires, the decay of cultures, the fall of kingdoms. These were mere episodes; when they ended, life went on. For the survivors, in fact, life may even have improved: a good case can be made for the view that the winnowing out of Europe's population by the Black Plague helped bring about the Renaissance. The scope of some of today's destructive possibilities would render such an outcome unlikely. Moreover, scientific opinion, which tended once to believe that life existed elsewhere through the universe, now seems inclined to the view that life is a one-time thing, unique to this planet in all of time and space, and so improbable an occurrence that the statistical odds of life emerging here would have had to have been stated beforehand as zero. If once destroyed, it would not come again.

We are not threatened by a simple, defined danger. If we were, then perhaps we could devise means to protect against it. Instead we are beset on all sides, and each preventive measure seems to generate a whole range of unexpected new perils, like dragon teeth sown against us. A well-known example is the development of DDT to curb plagues and famine; now it is DDT itself, according to the environmental movement, that has become the plague of the earth, threatening us with famine as well as suffocation. New evidence suggests that the environmentalists may be wrong; DDT may be broken down (by sunlight) before doing such harm; but the breaking down, we are told, in turn releases a poison that can be lethal. Here again the governments of nations are of little help. The problems are created by forces outside their territorial jurisdiction or over which they have no control; moreover their freedom of action is circumscribed by the vested interests of business and labor groups in practices and processes that create the problems. Other countries will not cooperate in situations where programs, though otherwise desirable, run counter to considerations of their perceived national interest. In addition, the growing range and scale of scientific, financial, and industrial activity have created an excessive number of demands on the governmental resources required for planning and regulation.

It is not only at the national level that governments seem unable to cope with their responsibilities. In the

United States (which seems to be the forerunner in exhibiting problems that stem from modern society), city and suburban governments have also become smaller than the scope of their problems.

The new shape of things, whether conceived of as the growth of the suburb or, alternatively, as the merger of expanding suburbs and cities into megalopolis, includes such harrowing problems as: the collapse of public transport under the enormous stresses it is forced to sustain now that commuting between cities and suburbs has become a mass movement; the loss of city tax revenues caused by the flight of upper- and middle-income groups to the suburbs, with consequent collapse of the facilities the city needs money to pay for, such as the school system, police, and utilities; overconcentration in the central city of the poor and the racial minorities, rendering the city the prime site and breeding ground of racial hatred, juvenile delinquency, chronic poverty, crime, congestion, pollution, and every form of human waste, loneliness, and despair. City governments are too small to reach into the suburbs to tax commuters to pay for municipal services; they are too small to legislate and regulate for the metropolitan areas, which are the real functional economic and social entities; and they are too small to override the myriad governmental authorities within the metropolitan regions to impose central direction.

As most people see it, however, city governments are also too large. Neighborhoods have lost the power to make decisions in matters that intimately affect their everyday life: for example, the regulation of automobile parking and traffic; the fixing of zoning rules with respect to the type of construction that can be undertaken; the formulation of policies concerning where children are to go to school and what and how they will be taught.

At all levels, then, governmental units seem to be of inappropriate size and of inadequate capabilities. They are not proportioned to the same scale and dimensions as the actual social entities, needs, and concerns for which they should be responsible.

This is a real problem, but it is not the whole problem. It is not enough to stop, as most political scientists do, at the observation that governments in the modern world are the wrong size. Stopping here reflects an unconscious assumption that any government that is the right size will succeed. It is one of those assumptions, of which we have spoken earlier, that require recognition and critical evaluation.

Indeed, the contemporary political experiences that have been recalled in the previous pages all have evoked responses based on an unexamined assumption that if a government is good enough, it can accomplish practically anything. Faced with the problems of the modern world, practical politicians as well as political theorists of all persuasions have proposed solutions of a governmental character. When Charles Merriam in essence proclaimed that there were no effective limits to what an efficient government could accomplish, the particular importance of his assertion was that *it articulated what almost everybody else unthinkingly assumed,* whatever their politics or their school of thought.

The experience of the contemporary world seems to

raise some question as to the validity of any such assumption. The governments of modern nations are failing to perform effectively even in areas that are properly proportioned to governmental size—something that suggests that size cannot be the whole of the problem.

Inflation is one such area. It may be the problem most responsible for the current distrust of government. It had been thought until recently that governments could control their domestic economic environments. Yet in country after country, inflation spirals out of control, with economically disastrous and socially disintegrating effects. Why? What has gone wrong?

Crime is another such area. Charles Merriam was able to write that it was no longer a problem and had been eliminated for the most part in modern societies. Now it is out of control, and fear dominates urban life. Why? What keeps the municipal and national governments of modern countries from preventing it?

Court calendars are so overcrowded that justice is either delayed or not done at all. Why? It is said that there is not enough money nowadays to support an effective judicial system; yet we are richer than ever before. Why is justice now beyond our financial means?

The governments of modern industrial states are poised to assume new responsibilities for the regulation of sophisticated emerging technologies and the preservation of the global environment, but they find themselves, instead, confronting failure at the most basic level: failure to police the cities, failure to enforce the laws, failure to pick up the garbage, failure to deliver the mail, and so on.

The spectacle of governments unable or unwilling to control events has its consequence in rising distrust of government as such. In a celebrated minimalist phrase, Lord Melbourne told Queen Victoria that "all government has to do is to prevent and punish crime"; but in contemporary America, the government cannot do even that. One result of this is a growing trend toward putting social services back into the private sector. The commercial success of private police and security forces and private postal services are symptomatic of the continuing disintegration of public functions.

Governments have never been cast for a more important role in world affairs than they have been today. The nineteenth-century growth of government—especially the change in function and structure of the executive— has been termed a "revolution"; yet it is dwarfed by the growth of this century, with governmental assumption of responsibility for health and welfare, of control over the economy, and of regulatory authority over a broad range of activities. The mushrooming scale and impact of scientific, technical, and industrial development seem to require, if anything, the assumption by governments of even more responsibility. All of life seems to be caught in what Professor MacIver called "the web of government." Yet just at this time the governments of the modern world seem to have broken down. Things are seen to be, and felt to be, out of control.

Throughout the industrial world people have lost faith

in their governments. Oddly, this has not led to a crisis of confidence in the institution of government itself—so powerful is the unconscious assumption that governmental techniques by themselves can solve all social problems. If city governments fail, it is thought to prove that metropolitan area governments will succeed; if national governments fail, it is thought to demonstrate that world government will succeed. These things do not necessarily follow. When communities fall apart, something more than the size of their political institutions is likely to have gone wrong; for institutions can easily be reshaped by constitutional lawyers if the need and the desire are there. The causes of social instability and disharmony must run deeper than that. Moreover, the processes of discord, once set in motion, create a momentum of their own that even a government of the appropriate size would be hard put to control.

The disintegration, disillusion, and despair feed upon themselves. As governments lose their grip, people react in ways that only make the situation worse. A case in point is the negative voting patterns that seem to be sweeping the democratic world. In election after election an agreement among a majority of the voters has failed to emerge, and issues have had to be decided by a mere plurality. The result is that minority government now is more the rule than the exception; and, by their nature, such governments lack the wide support necessary in order to do their job effectively. The large vote cast for protest groups, for fringe movements, and for third parties offering no conceivable alternative to the incumbents, underlines the fact that, in country after country, the electorate opposes the opposition as much as it does the administration. This unwillingness to join together in a popular majority makes it all the more likely that governments will perform in a way satisfactory to nobody. It is not merely an evidence of the failure of the political system; it is also a cause of partial paralysis in the system, precipitating its further failure.

The cycle of disillusion and disintegration is incarnate in separatism. The recent revival of claims to separate existence on behalf of Scotland, Wales, Cornwall, Quebec, Brittany, Languedoc, and others, whatever the validity of each claim, indicates that the respective national governments have seemed unresponsive to popular demands to such an extent that they are now regarded as alien. Separatism challenges, but also diminishes, the ability of national and federal governments to function effectively. In other words, separatist movements also follow the pattern of disintegration feeding upon itself: they are an evidence that existing governments to some extent have failed; but they are also a reason why such governments may fail even more.

A similar pattern is to be found in the typical forms of violence that disrupt the contemporary world. A rebellion against an unsatisfactory regime in order to install an acceptable one may be viewed in a constructive light; but the nihilism characteristic of current events, while directed against a failure of the political system, causes by its own methods a further breakdown of the system without putting something better in its place. Again, it is both a manifestation of failure and a cause of further failure. Riots, revolutions, and widespread acts of terrorism now seem to occur for no discernible reason and with no practically realizable objective in view. It is not an adequate explanation to point out that governmental units are of an inappropriate size, even though they are; the disorder and delirious violence of the contemporary world indicate that something else is fundamentally wrong as well.

Both the rhetoric and the reality of today's violence suggest its special character as an outburst of insurrection against any kind of system of modern life, and therefore against every form of authority and government. Now, as in the past, there are mass movements of violence aimed at achieving relatively tangible goals: jobs, or food, or the redistribution of land or wealth. Unlike past ages, however, ours also has given rise to other armed movements whose aims are vague to the point of meaninglessness. Their chief characteristic is their hopelessness. They challenge all governmental leadership because they make no demands that can be granted. Spokesmen for the Chinese cultural revolution seem to have been asking for a world in which students need no teachers and governments need no officials. Similarly, French student rioters in 1968 demanded an end to bureaucracy, to central decision making, and to hierarchies in trades and professions; more sweepingly, they also demanded that work should be made satisfying and meaningful, and that the consumer society should no longer be banal and without values. The problem of the de Gaulle government was how to surrender to such demands. The students had been carried away by a cause so hopeless that it could not succeed even if its opponents were prepared to capitulate. Such hopelessness is typical. The common characteristic of these modern mass movements is that they are self-defeating. They may bring down governments, but they bring themselves down in the process. In the United States summer rioters of the 1960s, in tantrums of rage and frustration, showed the pathological nature of their movement by their choice of target— the communities that they burnt to the ground were their own.

Senselessness also typifies the methods and stated aims of killers, kidnappers, hijackers, and extortionists whose professed political goals could not conceivably be achieved by the random terror and violence in which they indulge. Their methods lead nowhere; the only prospect they offer is violence without end.

The central new challenge to the institution of government arises from the inability of these groups and individuals to offer any serious alternative to the regimes that they oppose. If they could overthrow an existing government and take its place, then the violence might end and the effective government of society might resume. As it is, their ill-defined programs lead to perpetual terrorism and to increasing anarchy, thus enfeebling the existing governments but not replacing them. Indeed, if their slogans are to be believed, there are groups in many countries aiming at nothing more constructive than the general collapse of industrial civilization.

There are those who do not take the rhetoric seriously. They see the cultural revolution in China as a disguise for old-fashioned plotting by one leadership faction against another. They see the French student riots as a mass demand by young professionals for a larger share in the rewards of the consumer society they claim to despise; the fashionable language of alienation employed by the student leadership is seen as a cloak for the usual ambition of hungry young men to seize the power, position, and profits held by their elders. More persuasively, those who disregard the rhetoric see the political posturing of guerrilla terrorists as a fraud, masking ordinary criminals who seek to appear to be something better than common, but whose actions proclaim them to be the same as any other kind of lawbreakers.

In a sense, the explanations do not matter. The epidemic of violence is pathological even if it is being manipulated for allegedly rational motives. Moreover, the spreading chaos, the suffering and dislocation caused by orgies of destructiveness, and the undermining of all forms of authority and structure in the modern world are real. What is to be done about it?

For a democratic society, at least, military and police measures seem to prove ineffective unless carried so far as to destroy the society itself. That is what appears to have happened to Uruguay, once the stable, prosperous, model democracy of South America. Escalating its campaign to suppress the urban guerrilla group called Tupamaros, Uruguay succeeded in exterminating it by becoming a military dictatorship, her economy ruined and her society bitterly polarized. As at least one analyst has observed, it has become a dying country—a high price to have paid for preserving civic order. No viable solution has been found by other democratic societies, however; and therefore the disorder continues.

In the Soviet Union and in other dictatorships, police techniques seem to suppress effectively the currents of disorder. Yet suppression is not a long-term solution to a problem posed by genuine social forces. The price these dictatorships pay is in terms of structural instability. If the discontent finally finds expression, it will be in one explosion of accumulated force, shattering and perhaps even destroying the political system.

People have always assumed that governmental procedures can solve problems of this sort. It is one of the assumptions described in the first paragraph of this chapter: so unquestioned that it is rarely recognized. As observed earlier in the chapter, governments can now be seen to be the wrong size to deal with many such vital issues in the modern world; but to draw the usual conclusion that governments of the right size *necessarily* could deal with all the issues would be to make an argument based precisely on this unstated and unexamined assumption. As the evidence of inflation, crime, and rampant disorder in the modern world seems to show, this unspoken assumption is untrue; it appears that governments can do far less for us than political scientists and historians have previously led us to suppose.

Have we interpreted the evidence correctly? It relates to contemporary experience, and perhaps because of our proximity to it we have misperceived it, as we have misperceived so many currents of events in our time. Turning to historical evidence drawn from another period of widespread crisis, we find support for the interpretation. The evidentiary uses of historical analogy are complex and not without difficulty; historical experience, too, can be misperceived, and it is not intended here to assert otherwise. Inferences drawn from what we believe to have happened in the past cannot provide certainty; but they can tend to confirm similar inferences independently drawn from contemporary evidence. It is this sort of confirmation that is provided by the historical inquiry in the next chapter.

The period of crisis to which our own is there analogized is the decline of the ancient world and the fall of Rome. It is a period like our own in that governmental techniques proved unable to cope with a society that was coming apart. The inadequacy of the governmental mechanism, the sense of helplessness in the face of great problems and grave dangers, and the feeling of political and social disintegration give the modern world a certain resemblance to Rome in her final days. To that extent we are reliving the Roman experience, and there is a reason for the shivers-up-the-spine feeling that we have been here before.

The institution of government did not seem to require much critical assessment in 1945. Now, however, it does not seem to function satisfactorily; there are lapses and failures in important areas. The erosion of its authority adds a new dimension to the crisis of contemporary existence. The old problems have not gone away; political rivalries such as those of the United States with the Soviet Union and the Soviet Union with China continue; but to some extent they have been superseded by a wider peril. It is a peril that civilization supposedly had left behind it long ago. Not since the last days of the ancient world has complete social disintegration seemed to threaten. The modern world had not realized what it meant to undergo such an experience. Now, we do; and suddenly, across the gulf of 1,500 years, we understand the helpless despair of the last Romans as they ". . . lost all control of the vast machine."

2

A ROMAN ROAD

An appropriate monument to the special grandeur of ancient Roman government and to its distinctive genius is the remnant of its comprehensive network of highways, which continues to serve public needs even today. Surviving the ravages of time and history, throughout the lands that once formed its empire—in Britain, in continental Europe, in northern Africa, and in western Asia—traces still remain of roads that were constructed during the Roman administration of public affairs. In many of these lands the system of roads has never again been so good. In others, such as France, the system has been retained and improved; modern highways have been built on top of the ancient ones. Among the many pleasures of driving to the French Mediterranean is the knowledge that below the surface of the pavement lies a heritage of two thousand years, and that across the centuries, shades of the ancient world—poets and philosophers, consuls and senators, circus charioteers, and clanking legions on the march—have traveled along that same Roman road to the sea.

It is sometimes said that morally, socially, and politically we are also following the path of Rome. True, it is usually popularizers overstepping the bounds of their knowledge of history who say it; but the validity of a proposition cannot be judged by the company it keeps, and it is undeniably the case that there are similarities between some of the Roman experiences and some of our own. There are the obvious and frequently cited ones: the disintegration of family and religious ties, the spreading appeal of astrology and superstitions, the debasing of traditional intellectual and moral standards, and the debasing of the currency. Other parallels, although less often the subject of comment, are nevertheless germane. The great growth in the municipal population of Rome led to disturbance and turmoil not unlike the explosive social problems that have been created today by urbanization. The endemic, pervasive violence that became a feature of life in late republican Rome is indeed familiar in our own lives, as is the cancerous growth of bureaucracy that typified the empire. Furthermore, as in so many states in modern America, the Roman legislature was weighted in the rural interest by a system that deliberately put the chief political power in agrarian hands and subordinated the industrial population of the city. These things have parallels in other times as well; but in Rome they clustered together to form a disease of the body politic, and the danger is that they may do so with us as well. It is this that prompts an inquiry into the Roman experience to discover what bearing, if any, it has upon our own.

Alarmed, even as many people are alarmed today, by the loss of civic virtue, by the loss of concord and consensus, and by the loss of social cohesion and control, the orators of antiquity indulged in much the same kind of rhetoric that can be heard from hortatorians of our own time who urge a return to the ethical principles of the past. In other words, faced with some of the same problems, we say some of the same things about how to solve them. Our thinking is sufficiently similar to theirs that we often blunder in the same way that they did. Some speculative thinkers today, for example, misunderstand history in the same sort of way that Romans did. There are similarities between the ways in which the comparison with Rome is misused today in predicting the fate of the modern world and the errors made by early Romans in applying what they saw as patterns of past history to a vision of their own future. Those who argue that we cannot learn anything from the mistakes we observe in Roman history should at least admit that we can learn a great deal from the mistakes of Roman historians.

Commencing in the second century B.C., Romans claimed to see the decay of their civilization and its imminent and inevitable collapse. Their quasi-biological theory, borrowed from mysterious Etruria, was supported by observation of the supposed life cycles of empires to their east. These forebodings were based on the assumption that history has a design and is predictable; in this sense they can be compared to the morphological categorizations of Toynbee. They also are paralleled in modern times by the pessimism that characterized the turn-of-the-century and that found expression in Spenglerian theories of liberal-democratic decadence and

premonitions of imminent collapse. Of course, the prophets proved utterly wrong. Rome did not decay or decline
or collapse in the second century B.C.; far from it: she
went forward to greatness, glory, and empire. It was all
ahead of her. They had said it was the dusk before
twilight, but it turned out to be the dusk before dawn.

Rome did not go the way of Persia or Macedonia, and
we are not going to go the way of Rome. All that we
know for sure is that historical events are unique; the
problems, people, and situation are immensely different;
and whatever happens to us will be different in at least
some ways from what happened to anybody else.

What, then, have we to learn from a study of the
Roman experience? First of all, we can and should learn
what happened for its own sake. As Ferdinand Lot has
suggested, the collapse of the ancient world "is perhaps
the most important and most interesting problem of
universal history." Moreover, we learn from studying the
decline and fall of Rome how we, as progeny of the
European culture, came to be who we are and where we
are. Such is the historical vision with which Edward
Gibbon claimed to have been inspired as he sat amidst
the ruins of the Roman Capitol, watching Franciscan
monks sing vespers in what remained of the pagan
temple of Jupiter. To him the moving image was a
picture of the main event of the historical period under
consideration. He saw in it an embodiment of his
realization that the emergence of Christian Europe from
the declining, falling empire was the central episode in
European history. A study of it is therefore relevance

itself; for it shows us whence we came, and therefore helps us think about where we are and where we should be going.

A consideration of the empire's collapse helps, by analogy, to clarify an understanding of contemporary world events. We are confused, for example, by the sudden loss of American national security in the twentieth century; the Romans were even more confused by the crumbling of theirs. If we knew what caused the turn in their affairs, we might better understand what caused the turn in ours.

In its own time, Rome of the Caesars had been considered immortal. Its empire had endured so long that its subjects could not conceive of its ever coming to an end. Pagans believed that the rule of Rome would last forever, and Christians thought that it would endure until the coming of Antichrist and the Last Judgment. The collapse of the western empire, therefore, seemed incomprehensible. To such an extent do we share the same intellectual outlook that the fall of Rome remains incomprehensible—or, at any rate, uncomprehended—even today. The attempt to understand and explain it, which was begun contemporaneously by St. Augustine and his pagan opponents, has never ceased. The fall of Rome continues to haunt the imagination of the world. According to Santo Mazzarino, "Not only contemporary thought but also posterity has regarded this . . . as the archetype of cultural decline and as a warning which also contains the key for the interpretation of the *whole* of our history." Like the Romans, we are of the view that history has now become whole and universal. As Polybius

wrote with respect to the 140th Olympiad (220–217 B.C.),
". . . up to this time the world's history had been, so to
speak, a series of disconnected transactions, as widely
separated in their origin and in their results as in their
localities. But from this time forth History becomes a
connected whole. . . ."

At the very outset—in the work of St. Augustine—
what happened to Rome was seen, not as an isolated
event, but as a drama of universal history holding
universal meaning. It has been considered as such ever
since; and the seeing of it has enriched the intellectual
experience of mankind. To it we owe the expression of
valuable and important views, ranging from Augustine's
profound affirmation of belief to the enlightened skepticism of Edward Gibbon. Nor has its significance been
viewed exclusively in the context of religious or antireli-
gious thought: Montesquieu, for example, related it to
modern issues of politics and government in a way that is
permanently meaningful. As Geoffrey Barraclough has
written with respect to the crisis of the Roman Republic,
"For any one who believes in the 'relevance' or actuality
of history, there is less to be gained, in the present world,
from scrutinizing anxiously the origins of the Second
World War than from studying Caesar and the Roman
revolution, a revolution which may be paralleled sooner
than we think in our own society."

What do historians tell us were the causes of Rome's
fall? They tell us many things and they tell us nothing:
which is to say, many explanations have been offered, but
none has found general acceptance. Gibbon himself,
according to a recent analyst of his work, was confused in

his response: "In the first half of the *Decline and Fall* there are at least two dozen specific 'causes' given for the fall of Rome." Two centuries of scholarship have passed since Gibbon wrote, and yet even Michael Rostovtzeff, who came as close as anyone to succeeding in the endeavor, conceded that "None of the existing theories fully explains the problem of the decay of ancient civilization."

As will be seen, it is really that historians consistently attempt to answer the wrong question. Their question conceals the assumption, attacked in the previous chapter, that if a government is good enough it can accomplish anything. In fact, as will be indicated later in this chapter, the Roman experience contradicts any such assumption. The fall of Rome requires explanation only if the survival of Rome is considered to have been the normal and ordinary expectation under the circumstances. Quite the reverse seems to have been true. The question is not: Why did the Roman Empire cease to exist? Rather, it is: How did Rome, that improbable and improvised empire, manage to continue to exist for so long against such considerable odds? This question raises issues that are not merely of historical concern; they are also directly relevant to the great public questions of the contemporary world.

In its early days, Rome was a city-state; and from the very beginning there were indications that the city-state form of government would prove seriously inadequate. In it, religious, social, and political loyalties centered around a particular locality. Within that locality, its altars and its agora were the loci of its being. Except for cities in close physical proximity, there was no possibility of fusion or growth, for it was constitutionally difficult, if not impossible, for a city-state either voluntarily or through conquest to join another city-state to form a single, larger entity. Alliance with other city-states was possible, but (to use the language of corporate finance) not acquisition or merger. Thus the accumulation of enough power to create either unity or a permanent hegemony was prevented. The system of political organization conduced to a relatively even distribution of power and in turn to the kind of balance-of-power politics characterized by divisiveness, jealousy, envy, suspicion, constant watchfulness, and continual conflict.

In contrast, kingdoms, because they had no such limitations, were not inherently inhibited from expanding. In China, for example, during the first millennium B.C., one kingdom was able systematically to conquer all others and then lay the foundations for a national state. While geographical circumstances were, admittedly, favorable to Chinese unity, success in accomplishing unification had to do mostly with the fact that China had the type of political organization appropriate for the achievement of it.

Similarly in India, after the disappearance of the city-states and the invasion of the Aryans, a kingdom was able to expand its power and realize nationhood in the Mauryan Empire. Even the tribal and dynastic empires of the Eurasian land mass proved capable of expansion, but the city-states did not. In this sense the city-state was a historical regression, for it proved to be less flexible than the tribal type of organization that had preceded it.

The history of Sumer is the earliest political experience currently known to us (because it is the earliest civilization whose written records are available) and, already in that far-off time, the weakness in city-state organization can be seen. Five thousand years ago the Sumerian city-states began to lose their ability to maintain the requisite amount of peace, order, and security compatible with continued existence. Their territories and requirements started to overlap, and yet, although of a homogeneous culture, they were unable to coordinate their activities or to arrive at mutually agreeable solutions. Wracked by civic discord, they slid into chronic intercity warfare and entered into unstable, rapidly changing alliances with and against one another. Unable to deal on a united basis with common problems or with common enemies, they declined and then they fell, conquered in the twenty-third century B.C. by Sargon and the semitic northerners of Akkad.

Two millennia later the drama was replayed by the Greek civilization. After the empire of Cyrus and Darius was defeated by the ephemeral unity of Hellas, despite a common culture, common religion, common customs (which have been analogized to international law), and common interests, the Greek world of city-states tore itself apart in class conflict, civil war, and warfare between one city and another. These wars may have been the primary cause of the economic decline of the Greek world. Eventually, the city-states succumbed to Alexander and Macedon, foreshadowing the rise of Rome to future empire. As Werner Jaeger wrote:

. . . [T]hey had no political future. . . . The historical life of the city-state had come to an end, and no new artificial organization could replace it. . . . The fact is that the Greeks were unable to develop the feeling of nationhood, in the *political* sense, which would have enabled them to build up a nation-state. . . . In his *Politics* Aristotle declares that if the Greeks were united they could rule the world. But that idea entered the Greek mind only as an abstract philosophical problem.

For the Greeks as for the Sumerians (and later for the city-states of Renaissance Italy), the potential for unity was there, in the form of common culture and an inchoate sense of group solidarity (at least against outsiders); but this potential remained unrealized.

The city-state form of government was in crisis as soon as economic and political requirements outgrew the civic boundaries. Like the nation-states of today (a frequent and obvious analogy), the city-states had become inadequate to fulfill even the basic functions of government. It seemed that what was required was a higher and wider political authority, which would supersede the individual state in sovereignty. Unable to keep peace within and among themselves, and unable to unite for defense against common enemies or for the solution of common problems, they had need of a larger government to impose peace and law and make possible a settled civilization and a renewed prosperity. They needed a central government. Since they were unwilling to federate, they needed a conqueror. Rome, as we know, filled that role. It seemed to be a solution to the city-state problem; but, as will be suggested again later, it proved to be a false one. Rome did not prevent the fall of the ancient world; she merely postponed it. The contemporary importance of this observation is that it suggests that

a Roman solution may not be the proper one for us
either.

Stringfellow Barr has written that, "During its seven
and a quarter centuries of existence, Rome had learned
many important lessons, but she believed she had learned
one lesson above all others: that the only foundation for
law and order in the human community is the over-
powering force of government." Whether or not this is in
fact the lesson that she learned, it was certainly the lesson
that she taught.

Rome was able to conquer, to occupy, to police, and to
bring peace, law, and order by imposing her government;
but she was only able to do all of this at a cost that she
could not afford. Rome herself was only a city-state, and,
as such, she, too, had inadequate resources and was prey
to civil war and foreign war. In addition, her government, like that of other city-states, was narrowly based.
For her, the way up and the way down were one and the
same. Both the rise and the fall of Rome resulted from
living on a scale that was ultimately beyond her means in
order to support the professional, long-service army that
made her conquests possible. It is astonishing that she
was able to do so for as long as she did, but it is not in the
least surprising that she was not able to do it forever.

The professional army brought conquests and glory to
the Roman republic, but it also destroyed that republic.
A rootless army of the poor, owing loyalty to various
generals rather than to Rome, became the reality of
Roman politics. In defiance of the government, the army
followed rival commanders into a civil war that so utterly

destroyed the ruling autocracy that Sir Ronald Syme has described its convulsions as a revolution.

The professional army went on to create its own necessity. It conquered an area so vast that only a professional army could police it. It carried the empire so far that the last buffer-states were absorbed, leaving the Roman frontier face to face with fierce German and Iranian tribes that threatened invasions against which only a professional army could defend. As Rostovtzeff observed;

The new army owed its origin not merely to barbarian danger . . . but mainly . . . to the Roman Empire . . . the Roman world-state. Without such an army the world-state could not continue to exist, it was bound to fall to pieces. . . .

The army had to be permanent and had to be an army of professionals: no militia could defend the frontiers of the Roman state. The military technique of that age was too complicated to be learned in a short time. . . . If the army was to be a long-service army of professionals, it could not, as a rule, be levied compulsorily. . . . Men levied compulsorily would never make good professional soldiers, ready to devote their lives to the service. This being so, the army must be adequately paid. . . . Thus the expense of the army was a heavy burden on the finances of the state.

Indeed, from the beginning Roman power and Roman world-government were built on a false foundation, for they were only made possible by a professional army that the city-state ultimately could not support. In time of peace the receipts of the imperial government may have been sufficient; in time of war they were inadequate. Rome had invented a military technology too effective to abandon, yet too expensive to maintain. Furthermore, the uneven distribution of the booty of victory and the distortions and evils that it introduced into the economy also created new social tensions. These in turn increased the need for an army to preserve control.

The army came to political power in the civil wars, when it devoured the republic that had called it into being. Under the principate of Augustus and his successors, the army supported a monarchy. Later, dictatorship by the army became overt. Perhaps the principate should have made a greater effort to encourage the flourishing of those civil institutions that might have healed and united the Roman world. This might have resulted in a deeper sense of patriotism and civic virtue, which in turn might have obviated the need for a police-army. If this could have been achieved, military expenses might have been brought into line with available resources. Augustus, the first emperor, in some respects may have tried to do this. By creating an army-supported monarchy and by superimposing it upon the forcibly united city-states, he undertook to strengthen the civil institutions by a program of urbanization and by far-ranging improvements in the machinery of government.

The central flaw, however, remained. Without the spoils of victory the government lacked the money to pay for its army. As Rome came to the end of her frontier she was no longer financially able to support her army by conquest. The last major extensions by conquest of the Roman Empire were won in the reign of the emperor Trajan in the early second century A.D.; and they impoverished rather than rewarded the conquerors. As Rostovtzeff points out, "The successes of Trajan were

won at the cost of a severe strain on the whole Empire.
. . . The time was past when Roman wars paid for
themselves and when victories enriched the conquerors."
There is apparently strong evidence that at this point
requisitions were resorted to in order to meet the needs of
the army. Finally, however, the method that was employed was the debasing of the coinage by substituting
base metals for silver—inflation, as we would say.
Cheating of this kind is sooner or later found out; it is not
a workable approach over the long run. During the third
century the real value of Roman metal coinage fell to
about one-half of 1 percent of what it had been before the
inflation!

It is thus plain that there was in the organism of the Roman
state a deep-rooted trouble which could not be cured by
palliative measures. The state was constantly draining the
capital which was the life-blood of the Empire; all the
measures designed to restore the public finances were merely
repeated attempts to extract more money. . . . The great
Roman Empire was on the brink of returning to a natural
economy, because it could not acquire the requisite quantity of
good and stable currency.

Until recently this has been outside the experience of
the modern world, and therefore difficult for us to
imagine. The very terms *inflation* and *deflation,* which were
introduced in the latter half of the nineteenth century,
did not come into general use until the First World War.
Now these problems have become our own. Since the
Second World War, the Western industrial world has
witnessed an almost unbroken rise in prices and money
incomes. True, ours is largely a paper-money rather than

a coinage inflation, and the causes of our type of inflation are to some extent different, but, whatever may be the reason, we have now entered into the Roman experience of persistent, continuous, and apparently uncontrollable inflation as a way of life.

Rome's soldiers could not be fobbed off indefinitely by a government that had discredited its coinage and exhausted its credit. With silver coins depreciated, gold coins gone, and prices rising, the third century saw the anarchy of civil war, in which the army despoiled and destroyed the cities in order to meet the ravenous needs of the military budget. The cities were bankrupted; local self-government was destroyed; in the end there was a "gradual relapse . . . to very primitive forms of economic life, into an almost pure 'house-economy.' The cities, which had created and sustained the higher forms of economic life, gradually decayed, and the majority of them practically disappeared from the face of the earth."

The last emperors, whatever they themselves might have believed, were playing out a losing hand.

They took over a heavy heritage from the third century, to which they had to conform. In this heritage there was almost nothing positive except the fact of the existence of the Empire with all its natural resources. The men who inhabited it had utterly lost their balance. Hatred and envy reigned everywhere: the peasants hated the landowners and the officials, the city proletariat hated the city bourgeoisie, the army was hated by everybody, even by the peasants. The Christians were abhorred and persecuted by the heathens, who regarded them as a gang of criminals bent on undermining the state. Work was disorganized and productivity was declining; commerce was ruined by the insecurity of the sea and the roads; industry could not prosper, since the market for industrial products was steadily contracting and the purchasing power of the population diminishing; agriculture passed through a terrible crisis, for the decay of commerce and industry deprived it of the capital which it needed, and the heavy demands of the state robbed it of labor and of the largest part of its products. Prices constantly rose, and the value of the currency depreciated at an unprecedented rate. The ancient system of taxation had been shattered and no new system was devised. The relations between the state and the taxpayer were based on more or less organized robbery: forced work, forced deliveries, forced loans or gifts were the order of the day. . . .

. . . the bureaucracy gradually became utterly corrupt and dishonest and at the same time comparatively inefficient. . . .

To escape taxes landowners fled to the cities, even as today the owners and functionaries of industry flee to the suburbs. To tax and to requisition the government had to be able to find everyone. The solution of Diocletian was to freeze everyone permanently in his place of residence. "A wave of resignation spread over the Roman Empire. It was useless to fight, better to submit and bear silently the burden of life with the hope of finding a better life—after death." All of this was to enable the emperors to pay for the army in order to save the empire, which the army had created. However, "they never asked whether it was worth while to save the Roman Empire in order to make it a vast prison . . ." for those who lived in it.

In retrospect it seems that the future dilemma of the ancient Mediterranean world should have become clear in the fifth century B.C. We find in Thucydides the "concept that settled life and material progress are

possible only through political unification, which in
practice meant forcible control by some central authority." Yet, we also find in Thucydides an account of the
cruelty of Greek to Greek, the envy and hatred of class
for class and city for city, the brutalization of character,
and the erosion of ethical standards. All of these deterio-
rating tendencies not only required the imposition of
forcible control, but also rendered such control unaf-
fordably expensive to impose.

We would surely find ourselves in a similar situation
today if we attempted to impose a global government on
a world not yet ready for it. The same hatreds and
conflicts that lead us to think in terms of a governmental
solution would compel a worldwide authority to maintain armed forces on a scale so vast as to prove crushingly
expensive. At the present time the American military
budget is enormous; yet it would be dwarfed by the cost
of a world army sufficiently strong to coerce both the
United States and the Soviet Union. The world would
sink under the weight of its military costs, even as Rome
did. A powerful world army without national loyalties
might well make the government its pawn; here, too, the
Roman precedent augurs ill. The Roman experience also
suggests that the institution of overarching government
would not erase the national and ideological conflicts
that divide and trouble the world; it suggests that the
conflicts would merely assume the form of civil war
rather than national war.

In terms of their own world, Sallust and Julius Caesar
apparently believed that only civil war could finally
destroy Rome. It can well be argued that in the end they

were correct: the civil wars of the first century B.C.
destroyed the republic, and those of the third century A.D.
destroyed the empire, even as the fifth-century civil war
of Hellas destroyed classical Greece. So, too, did the 1914
war and its sequel (which some saw even at its outset as
the civil war of Europe) destroy the European world-em-
pire. Sallust and Caesar were correct in an even larger
sense. It was the disposition to civil war—the tendency to
strife, hatred, and envy, and the lack of solidarity and
patriotism—that made the population of the Roman
Empire ungovernable except by a military force so
overwhelming as to be financially ruinous.

Rostovtzeff has reasoned that the empire's weakest
feature was not maladministration nor even the burden
of its military budget; it was, in his view, the frailty of the
economic foundation on which the empire rested. He
argued that the economic life of the empire was not
progressive enough, to bear the heavy burden of maintaining itself as a single political unit.

This explanation has now become common and is
echoed in many otherwise admirable studies. The empire, they claim, lacked the resources to pay for the costs
of centralization. This explanation, however, seems to
place the emphasis of inquiry on the wrong side. It seems
to ask why Rome was not progressive enough to summon
up vast new financial resources that had not previously
existed. But why were they needed? The question is
really why the burden of maintaining a single political
unit was so heavy. Why were vast new resources necessary for centralization? Why, in other words, were the
people who inhabited the empire unwilling or unable to

live and work together in harmony and unforced cooperation?

Julius Caesar, "the sole creative genius produced by Rome, and the last produced by the ancient world," might perhaps have solved the problem had he not been assassinated. There have been many conflicting interpretations of Caesar's policy, in our day as well as in his own. Nobody can say with certainty what was in Caesar's mind or what he would have done. It seems probable, however, that Caesar's intention was to expand the social basis of the Roman polity. Theodor Mommsen, the German scholar who was perhaps the greatest historian of the Roman republic, interpreted Caesar's politics in this fashion. Even if it seems at times that he has made Caesar into an enlightened nationalist of the nineteenth century, suspiciously like himself, Mommsen's view is persuasive and remains influential. If his view was correct, then Caesar's was the program of the future. Other Roman politicians saw the situation of their republican city-empire in terms of an unwise abandonment of ancient institutions, practices, and modes of conduct and thought; for them the question was how to return to a more perfect yesterday. Mommsen's Caesar took the opposite position: he proposed to throw off the shackles of an obsolete past and create new political and social realities that would be better adapted to the needs and circumstances of the world in which he lived and better able to realize the possibilities of the future. His program, as so conceived, was modernism itself. Caesar was an aristocrat who led the party of democracy and who proposed a program of unification. His ideas apparently went beyond the known alternatives of city-state or empire. His concept, which was only achieved more than a thousand years later, was something akin to the national state, with all that it implies in terms of broad-based loyalty, group solidarity, social cohesion, reconciliation, and patriotism. Only such a program of changing the realities of the Roman world could have achieved success.

Some have suggested that the ancient world failed because it did not think of the theory of representative government. Yet the fact is that it did think of the idea; the failure to put it to much use was symptomatic of a deeper problem. The cause of failure was clearly not inadequacy of the system of government, for we know that under far less adequate systems of government many countries have long survived.

Indeed, the point about Roman government is that it was so good. That is one reason why it has been so widely studied and copied. The principles of Roman government and the maxims of her legal system are right reason itself. They continue to inspire even our own institutions and those of others who, like ourselves, are widely separated from Rome in place and time.

A tale from the far ends of Eurasia provides striking evidence of the excellence of Roman government. Some two thousand years ago a group of Roman legionnaires, campaigning in the Middle East against the empire of the Parthians, were captured by their enemies and taken prisoner. Evidence that has only recently come to light suggests that some of the Roman prisoners managed to escape and make their way east, where they seem to have taken service with the Mongolian Huns. The evidence further suggests that, nearly two decades later, 145 of these Romans were again taken prisoner, this time by the Chinese. Apparently the Romans then served as mercenaries in the Chinese army and were rewarded by being allowed to settle and found their own city in China. To this city, founded in about 5 A.D., they gave the name of Rome (in its Chinese translation: Li-jien). It now appears that the city was organized by them on a Roman model and that it endured as such for over seven centuries, until it was destroyed by a foreign invasion. The continuity and survival of Roman governmental institutions for so long and in such an alien climate attests to the powerful hold and attraction that they exerted. So far as we know, nothing forced the citizens of Li-jien to govern themselves in the Roman fashion or to apply to themselves the tenets of Roman jurisprudence. If anything, the social pressures in China would presumably have dictated against this. Moreover, the citizens of Li-jien must have become increasingly Chinese as a result of intermarriage. Yet century after century they apparently chose to continue conforming to the patterns of Roman government. Any type of government that can prove so satisfactory and durable, even in such adverse and unfamiliar circumstances, must be outstandingly good.

Not merely was Rome a model of good government; she was also its pure example. On analysis, it appears that the western empire was little else than a form of government. It was not like other empires. It was not one people ruling other peoples. It was not an Italian

occupation of the Mediterranean world. The extraordinary thing was that the peoples of the empire imposed its
rule upon themselves in order to receive the benefits of
the Roman type of government. By the second century
there were for all practical purposes no Italians in the
Roman army—probably less than 1 percent—and the
army, it will be remembered, was more than a military
force; it was also in large part the administrative system,
the judicial system, and the police system of the empire.
Starting with Trajan, the emperors, as well as the army,
were increasingly non-Italian too. This means that the
empire ruled and policed itself at its own expense and
remitted the profits to Rome. The Roman political
system was so admirable that Spanish emperors, Syrian
ministers, Serbian generals, and German soldiers combined with one another to impose it upon their own
nations and were willing to pay Rome for the privilege of
doing so. Roman procedures were learned and followed.
It was like a modern commercial franchise operation; it
was as though Rome were selling the franchise on
government to the peoples of the empire. The weakness
in this rational arrangement was that it did not rest on
feeling. It was a system that appealed to the head but not
to the heart.

As A. H. M. Jones commented, "No one who reads the
scanty records of the western empire can fail to be struck
by the apathy of the Roman population from the highest
to the lowest. . . . Provincials were profoundly grateful to
the Empire for protecting them from the barbarians and
maintaining internal security, and thus enabling them to
enjoy and develop the amenities of civilized life in peace.

But they felt no active loyalty, no obligation to help the emperor in his task." There was no sense of belonging to one common group—and it is precisely the common group sense that calls forth acts of patriotism. The inhabitants of the empire were merely diverse peoples living under the same authority. The empire was a jurisdiction rather than a nation. Rome was the extraordinary instance of a government lacking a political entity: it was a government without a country.

When Alaric sacked Rome in 410 A.D., there was no effective army to bar his way: the truly Roman army had disappeared centuries before. The defenders of the city were feeble. There was no patriotic citizenry to stand against the Huns, no Horatius at the bridge, as would have been the case in republican days. All that had protected Rome and prevented rapacious raids before Alaric was the fear that her former greatness had inspired in others. For all practical purposes the legions were long since gone. Once the raid had occurred, it suddenly became clear that only ghosts and memories had really stood between Alaric's hordes and the riches of the Eternal City.

What Rome had lost through the ages was the special feeling of loyalty to a political group that expresses itself in the form of patriotism. The need for nationality—otherwise stated, for a sense of community—is therefore a fundamental lesson to be learned from the Roman experience. Without it, Rome's long-service army had to be a mercenary army; and, as the modern world learned by itself in the wars of the French Revolution, mercenaries are useless against a long-service citizen army.

The invention of new military technology enabled Rome to overcome the limitations of city-state government to the extent that it allowed her to conquer her neighbors. Neither her military prowess nor her development of the best of governments, however, allowed her to overcome the limitations imposed by city-state loyalties so she could *consolidate* her conquests. The deep and passionate loyalties that citizens of the ancient Mediterranean world felt toward their respective cities were not transferred to the wider, all-encompassing entity of the empire. Old allegiances were shaken or shattered by the Roman conquest, but new ones did not arise to replace them. Looking back, it can now be seen that the Roman solution to the crisis of city-state politics was a false one because it was narrowly military and governmental. A successful solution would have had to be broadly based in a developed or developing sense of community.

How do we know that the lack of a sense of community dooms a government to failure? The Roman experience has been considered at such length largely because it constitutes a historical analogy tending to establish the truth of the proposition that such a sense of community *is* necessary. The outbreak of ruinous and sanguinary civil wars, the failure of the citizen body to rise up and repel the Hunnic hordes, and the constant need for an excessively expensive mercenary army are persuasive evidence that an active sense of community did not exist in the western empire. They are also among the major reasons why Rome could not continue to exist, despite its excellence as a government: because it was precisely her inability to create a feeling of group loyalty, such as ethnic groups express through patriotism, that was the downfall of Rome.

The proposition that a sense of community is essential to successful government is also supported by historical analogies of a converse sort. Empires and kingdoms that might not otherwise have endured have survived through the development of ethnic loyalty. Thus the empire which Rome created in the East lasted for a thousand years after Alaric sacked Rome; and it can be argued with much reason that the secret of Byzantium's success was her Greek ethnic basis. Another example that is especially pertinent is the empire that Alexander's general, Seleucus, carved out for himself in Asia; unlike the Roman leaders, Seleucus seems to have recognized that the lack of group loyalty was a fatal deficiency, and therefore he set out to supply it when he found it missing. "[T]o Seleucus a strong state meant the support of his own people. . . . The Seleucid idea was to give to the framework of their empire substance and strength by filling it out with Greeks; Greeks were to supply its living tissue. . . . The Greek settlement of Asia was one of the most amazing works which the ancient world ever saw, for . . . it was undertaken deliberately. . . ." It worked in the way in which it was intended; for ". . . the abiding loyalty of the . . . settlers to the person of the reigning Seleucid became notorious," and it seems to have been one of the chief reasons the Seleucid empire flourished, despite its motley character.

The contrasting examples of the Roman, Byzantine, and Seleucid empires demonstrate that active community loyalty is essential if a government is to successfully

meet severe challenges over a long period of time. It is
needed in order to ward off disasters and also to survive
the disasters if they occur. Thus, without an ethnic basis
there is no recovery from conquest. Take, for example,
the difference between what happened to the civilizations
of Rome and of China. It may be true, as Mark Elvin
recently argued, that the reason China continued to
defeat the barbarians—while Rome in the end did
not—was that China, unlike Rome, kept sufficiently
ahead of her opponents in various technical skills.
However, this cannot be the explanation of why one
empire survived and the other did not. China too was
eventually conquered by nomad hordes, not once but
repeatedly; but China remained China because she was
populated by ethnic Chinese. Rome was conquered only
once by nomad hordes, but it was an event that
permanently marked the end of her history. This was
because the people who inhabited the area between
Britain and Syria were not ethnic Romans: they were
merely for a time subject to Roman government. Some
Roman colonization of the empire did take place, but it
was inadequate to make the empire a nation in any real
sense.

Observers, drawing parallels, have seen in the dying
agony of the ancient world a crisis of political forms. It
was not that; it was a crisis of political substance. The
analogy often and eloquently drawn is that the ancient
world, like ours, was in need of wider political authority.
On the contrary: authority was then too wide to be
supported; it was wider than the real social-political
entities of its time. If we were to pursue the analogy in

practice at this time, by successfully enlarging the scope of our government to embrace the entire globe, we would merely be courting another decline and fall. The world we would try to govern lacks a common patriotism; it would therefore prove to be as ungovernable as did the Roman world. It seems to be true that only a worldwide authority could deal with the problems and opportunities of modern times on a fully adequate basis; but, unfortunately for us, the structure of political loyalties in the world today places such a solution out of reach at the present time. Nationalism is deeply and passionately felt, even though it can be shown that objective circumstances have made it dangerously obsolete.

It is a Roman mistake to think that, either then or now, it was or is sufficient to fit the size of a government to the size of the problems with which it must deal. There is a third element that must also fit, and that is the size of the group entity that evokes genuine and positive loyalty. It must correspond to the size of the government if the government is to succeed.

We are told nowadays that a world state, a world government, a world constitution, could constitute the salvation of a world threatened by national rivalry and nuclear destruction. The experience of Rome with "world" government suggests that this is not in fact a viable alternative: "this machinery . . . was 'too vast, too scientific, too complicated' and could not take the place of national spirit. . . ."

The actual or potential scope of national feeling must be enlarged before an expanded government can effectively or usefully function. It is not an easy thing to accomplish; yet it may not be an impossible one. A plausible approach to the achievement of such an enlargement is the functionalistic program of David Mitrany, as modified by Hans Morgenthau. It calls for patient diplomacy aimed at minimizing national differences, so that the interests that unite can be seen to be greater than the conflicts that divide. When such a change in political perception occurs, then enlarged groupings can be formed with a unity of purpose of the sort hitherto found only in wartime alliances. Within the framework of such unity, functional agencies can then deal on a transnational basis with the satisfaction of common needs. Ultimately, if such agencies were of sufficient importance in daily life, the peoples in question might develop loyalties to these institutions and to the enlarged community of which they would be the agency; and such loyalties might supersede national loyalties. Thus in the end both the community and its government could be enlarged.

It is not, as has been said, an easy program to accomplish, nor can it be quickly done. Its major merit is that there seems to be no equally plausible alternative available to us.

The Roman experience seems to show that some program of this sort is a prerequisite to the successful enlargement of the ambit of governmental authority in the world. Unlike the Roman government, our national governments today are more correctly proportioned to the loyalties of the communities they serve; but, also unlike the Roman government, they are too small to function adequately in the changed circumstances of the world in which they exist. Expanding the scope of the governments to coincide with the size of their task—without also expanding the scope of the communities over which they have jurisdiction—would be following the Roman road to failure.

Another aspect of the Roman experience, however, suggests that even the enlarged government of an enlarged community would not provide a fully adequate cure for the political ills of our time. In this the Roman experience confirms the contemporary experience discussed in the previous chapter. Many of Rome's symptoms of social disorder were similar to our own. This suggests that we may be suffering from the same disease. In retrospect we can see that the Roman malady was a lack of a sense of community. This helps us see that it is probably a lack of community feeling that troubles us too. We can see that the cure, for Rome, would have been the development of a Roman nationality. Yet our governments today do have a national basis; and we seem to suffer from the lack of community nonetheless. Thus a process of reasoning from the Roman comparison seems to indicate that the inferences drawn from contemporary events at the end of the last chapter were correct: that even when the community and its government are the right size, some new force in the modern world is corroding the sense of community and, therefore, destroying the ability of governments to govern.

Improving the quality of our governments is not a complete answer; the Roman experience shows that it is not. Roman government failed even though it was a model of excellence. Excellence proved to be irrelevant.

Government alone—even the best government the world had known—was insufficient.

The Romans relied too heavily upon the effectiveness of their government. So do we upon our own. As the problems of the modern world accumulate, we are told that our governments can solve them. The history of Rome shows that such a solution is at best incomplete: it shows that government alone is not enough.

What more is needed? What are the conditions under which governments can effectively function? Answers to questions that are so far-reaching require an equally broad understanding of the essential nature and inherent limitations of political institutions. They also call for a review of the social context in which such institutions operate.

We are driven, then, back to a consideration of basic matters. What is a government? What is its proper function? What can it do and what can it not do? Are there any other institutions that can take its place? In quiet, uneventful times people apparently delude themselves into believing that they have outgrown the need to think about these introductory questions and concepts in political science. The turbulence of the present century has deprived us of any such luxury. The continuing political crises of our time make us return to a consideration of what is genuinely fundamental and what is not. They bring us back to an elementary investigation of governmental institutions and their role, and to the sort of general, overall questions with which such a survey is necessarily concerned. The eventfulness of the twentieth century has made freshmen of us all.

3

DEFINING THE
FUNCTION OF
GOVERNMENT

How should we go about investigating the basic characteristic that defines the institution of government across
the whole range of space and time? A plausible answer is
that it can best be done by examining how and why the
institution first came into existence. Following in the
footsteps of Aristotle, classical political scientists sought to
explain the nature and function of government in terms
of its origins, for, "He who thus considers things in their
first growth and origin, whether a state or anything else,
will obtain the clearest view of them." Yet we still know
very little about the origins of government, and the
theorists who formerly dealt with these questions knew
nothing at all about it—or less than nothing, for the
scientific views upon which they based their theories are
now known to be false. Nonetheless the Aristotelian
approach still seems to afford the best chance of arriving
at a true understanding of the matter.

Those who have taken the opposite approach, attempting to explain the function of government in the

light of today's institutions, to a great extent have also been misled. As Aristotle observed with respect to city-states, institutions created for one reason may flourish for quite different reasons. Existing governments perform many functions that have little to do with the reasons for which governments came into existence. In the course of time, purposes served by ancient governments have been abandoned, while modern governments have expanded their functions, serving purposes unthought of in ancient times. Those who restrict their studies to modern governments cannot know which of these purposes have *always* been served by governments, or *must* always be served by them.

Until now, explanations of the nature and function of government have been flawed and inadequate for reasons of this sort. Either they have rested on faulty science, or they have reflected the partial and provincial view that all governments and societies must have been like those we know.

A fully adequate explanation of what governments necessarily and essentially do, therefore, has not yet been found; and an attempt will be made in this chapter to supply one. An empirical test of the adequacy of any such explanation is whether the denominator which it offers is in fact common to all governments of which we can learn. If any government can be found, anywhere or anytime, that did not fulfill the function in terms of which government is explained, then the explanation fails.

This requires, as has been said, a reconnaissance of the whole spectrum of governments that the world has known. The scope of the enterprise is immense. There-fore, the view that we take of it first must be placed in proper perspective, because if we think of governments in far-off times in our own terms, we will misunderstand them and the role they played in society. Difficult though it is to do it, they must be understood in their own terms. More difficult still, we then must try to fit them and ourselves into the overall scheme of things, as such a scheme might be perceived by an observer who stood above us all. The problems to which this gives rise are those of proper focus; and of course they must be considered carefully before we appropriately can con-sider anything else.

The narrow range of our experience within historical times tends to limit our outlook in ways that we must strive to overcome by clearly recognizing them. The earliest governments of which we have actual knowledge were the product of an agricultural revolution that took place in at least two or three separate parts of the world only ten or fifteen thousand years ago, and which resulted in a settling down of much of the human race after millions of years of nomadic wandering. The Ice Ages had melted into the past, the world basked in its springtime, and the domestication of plants and animals made it feasible for the first time to inhabit a fixed location. The settlement of the earth resulted in villages and, eventually, in cities, which became the market centers of an agricultural economy. Civilization, of course, derives from the Greek word for city; this agriculturally based civilization was therefore the first civilization there had ever been. Seen from this perspective, the industrial civilization in which we live is only the second civilization that the earth has known. This is one of the reasons why it is difficult for us to place our view of government-in-human-affairs in proper focus: our form of life is a recent novelty on the planet.

It is a distortion of perspective to think that the civilized governments of classical, medieval, and modern times, which form the exclusive subject of traditional political studies, are really the whole of political history. In point of time they occupy a quite minor portion of human history—in numerical terms, less than one percent, perhaps even an insignificant fraction of one percent. Most of human existence has been unsettled and uncivilized, and for the most part governments have been quite different from our own. The organized types of government we now have are characteristic of settled and more-or-less urban societies, the earliest forerunners of which are thought unlikely to be much older than 8000 B.C. If man-like creatures have really inhabited the earth for millions of years, then, by comparison, from that time perspective, the organized types of government some parts of the world have known for ten thousand years were only developed this morning. Civilized government has not been universal even within that ten thousand years; primitive peoples continue to exist even today.

Moreover, the patterns and perceptions of existence have changed, not merely in the large framework of human history, but also in the limited framework of civilization's ten thousand years. The structure of life has changed: for example, in the Bronze Age average life expectancy was short—perhaps only about eighteen years—and that would make their existence much different from ours today. The structure of thought has changed, too: modern historians have only just begun to grapple with the problem of understanding people who felt things in a different sort of way, who relied more than we do on senses other than vision, and whose time perception was vague in terms of years, but more acute than ours in terms of seasonal change and the difference between day and night.

The conflicts that formed the great issues of politics also were different in other times. The ascent to civilization was the step up from nomadism to village agriculture. It is precisely the uncertainty, the difficulty, and the contesting of that change that formed the theme of history during the agricultural civilization, stretching from the founding of Jericho to the fall of the two Roman empires and the collapse of medieval China. The history of the ancient world was therefore "about" an issue that has neither relevance nor importance in today's industrial civilization. It was about the hazardous effort to achieve civilization (in the sense of "the settled life"). It was about the struggle against nature, an enterprise the outcome of which was far from certain: the Egyptians and the Mesopotamians conquered the flood, but the Indus valley civilization, with its glorious cities Mohenjo-daro and Harappa, seems to have succumbed to it. It was about the wars between the nomads and those who had settled: the Roman empires of East and West both, in the end, fell to the nomads; China fell to them repeatedly; and only by luck did medieval Europe escape a Mongol conquest. Agricultural settlements, villages, and cities were created with great effort; they existed in constant peril from nature and the nomad hordes; and in the end they decayed and were swept away by nomad conquest or were covered over by sand.

"Civilization may be either desert (Bedouin) civilization. . . . Or it may be sedentary civilization as found in cities, villages, towns, and small communities. . . ." So wrote Ibn Khaldun in the fourteenth century, establishing the apparently eternal polarity of which he became the sociologist and philosopher. In their opposed relationship was to be found the pattern of history as it then was throughout Eurasia. In it he found the framework for a discussion of the basic political issues of the world he knew—a world, as we can now see, that lasted for about ninety-five hundred years. A comprehensive description of government must take account of the relevance of what he wrote in its own context and of its irrelevance outside of that context.

Not merely were the substantive issues of politics and government different in other times, but the way in which people thought about them differed as well. The medieval conception, for example, is murky to us, yet clear enough in its own time. It saw the function of government as giving judgment; its role was essentially judicial. This is clarified for us only when we realize that to people in medieval times the law was not primarily something created or enforced by them, but something that existed as part of the national or local life. In such a society the role of government appears to have been to interpret the law, rather than to enact it or to secure obedience to it. Government was thought of as a modest intermediary.

This relates to what well may be the most important difference between the way in which the modern world has thought about government for the past few hundred years and the way in which it was thought about before modern times, and indeed ever since time began for the human race. The role of government for much of human history has been to act as interpreter in the dialogue between man and the universe; and as such, it was steeped in magic, in superstition, or in religion. On behalf of their people, leaders of tribes and nations propitiated the elements, invoked spirits, or prayed to the gods; on behalf of the elements, spirits, or gods, the leaders gave instruction and direction to their people. Indeed, the concept of government leadership drawing its authority from mysterious, supernatural, or sacred sources has continued into modern times, for until very recently the divine right of kings was a seriously believed theory.

"In the beginning religion was everything," as one student of government has observed—which overstates the case, but in the right direction. Religion was the matrix and context of thought. The gods presided over the hunting of animals, the planting of food, and the movement of peoples. When the human race eventually came to create cities and consequently civilization, this too was an act of religion, far removed from the secular orientation of current urban studies. As Fustel de Coulanges wrote of the ceremonies of civic foundation:

These usages show clearly what a city was in the opinion of the ancients. Surrounded by a sacred enclosure, and extending around an altar, it was the religious abode of gods and citizens. Livy said of Rome, "There is not a place in this city which is not impregnated with religion, and which is not occupied by some divinity. The gods inhabit it." What Livy said of Rome any man might say of his own city. . . . [E]very city might be called holy.

For many ages religion was the matrix of law and government. Political life continued to be generally conceived in religious terms until quite recently. In medieval Europe political thought was a system of values and obligations deriving from the Christian faith. There are still remnants of the religious connection in governmental concerns today—among others, in the law of marriage and divorce. Not only in the Christian world and in the world of Islam are such remains to be found. Marxist, Leninist, and Maoist theories of government, current in the contemporary world, can also be seen as conceptions analogous to the religious conception of government.

Machiavelli is often called the gateway to the modern world because he engaged in secular political thought. His works have been interpreted through the years in many very different ways, but there is no mistaking the revolution he started by separating politics from religion. For us one of the problems is to comprehend the mental processes of those who lived before this revolution (which, in the immense time-perspective of history, means almost everybody except ourselves). Fortunately, the disciplines of academic understanding have expanded in recent times so as to make it easier for us to do so.

Modern science and scholarship have given us a chance, denied to our ancestors, to look before and beyond ourselves. In the last two centuries, anthropologists have opened up a whole panorama of previously unknown cultures for our comprehension, and thereby have extended vastly the range of possibilities that can be seen to be available to human societies. In comparison, the traditional theories of political science, based as they were upon only the political experience of civilized society, have come to appear narrow and rigid.

This is particularly true of theories about the nature and function of governmental processes. According to the most persuasive anthropological views, no society exists without government; and yet, as Austin Ranney has observed, "one of the most striking facts about actual governments, past and present, is that no two have been exactly alike." Moreover, each government is in some senses different at different points in time: the government of the United States in 1974, for example, is in many ways different from the government of the United States in 1800. Since there have been an immense number of societies in the world, and each one of them has had a somewhat different kind of government, and since each government in turn differs from its previous self as it progresses in time, the catalogue of governmental differences is of a scope that is almost unimaginably vast. Thus the identification of the function common to all governments is a challenging enterprise.

The definitions of the function of government that have been offered up until now have become obsolete as a result of this expansion of the scope of the inquiry. A clear example of this is the case of the Marxist definition, which was based on an anthropology that has since been superseded. Marx accepted the anthropological view of his day that society originally was communistic and without government. His theory was that government exists as the agency of class warfare and would necessarily disappear as society reverted to its original state of classlessness. However, now that anthropologists have shown that all societies do have governments (including primitive societies that do not have social classes), the Marxist theory is invalidated. By definition, the government of a classless society cannot be engaged in class warfare; it must be doing something else. If it does not engage in class warfare, then the waging of class warfare cannot be the function that defines government.

The Marxist view is not the only one that has been invalidated by the new consciousness of the wide range of possibilities available to society. All of the standard views, it now can be seen, relate to the government of a particular society or group of societies rather than to governmental processes in the life of mankind as a whole. It becomes increasingly more clear that the usual procedure of political scientists in every age has been to define government in terms of the functions important to their own society, while ignoring the existence of societies for whom such functions are not important and for whom they therefore are not performed. The inappropriateness of such a technique is all the more apparent as we become aware of the immense divergences among societies with respect to their modes of existence as a group.

Governments have organized many types of group

activity; it has been usual to choose particular aspects of group activity and claim that *these* are the *real* reason for the existence of government. Preserving law and order is an example; because it seems to be so basic to any organized regime, political philosophers of many societies have seen in it the function that defined government. It is now well known, however, that there are tribes in which the government does not undertake such protection, but concerns itself with other things; feuds and self-help instead are the rule. Therefore even so basic and widely performed a function as the imposition of law and order does not define government.

At the other extreme, the function of government has been defined in highly sophisticated terms by some of the outstanding representatives of the Chicago school of political scientists. Children of the consumer age, children of the computer age, David Easton and Gabriel A. Almond speak of government functions in terms of satisfying demands and in terms of input and output. They are far from the tribes of the primeval jungle.

There are governments that do almost nothing and governments that do almost everything. The anthropologist Lucy Mair describes a government, consisting only of the two eldest members of the tribe, that has the sole and exclusive function of cursing wrongdoers. At the other extreme, an inventory of governmental activities in the United States published in 1947 listed almost four hundred services performed by American units of government. The objective must be to discover what these two governments have in common.

A recent textbook expresses a standard outlook based on an observation of modern governments, when it describes the minimum objectives of government as follows:

1. the security of people from arbitrary assault and annoyance by other citizens;
2. the security of the goods of people from damage and theft by other citizens;
3. the security of people and their goods from hurtful actions by other states;
4. the settlement of disputes between citizens;
5. the improvement of the general well-being of the citizens.

This, it is fair to say, represents the reference-book or textbook point of view. The language varies from text to text, but the substantive doctrine is much the same.

A less neutral formulation was proposed by Charles Merriam, who surveyed the political history of mankind and wrote with comprehensive intent: "The ends and purposes of government, much discussed by men of all ages, may be simply stated as follows: (i) external security, (ii) internal order, (iii) justice, (iv) general welfare, and (v) freedom." This is a humane and decent man's list of what a government ought to do; but quite apart from the ambiguity of "purpose" (whose?) and the vagueness of "general welfare" (would it have included participation in the Crusades in the thirteenth century, or in space exploration in the twentieth century?), it does not describe what governments have actually done. None

of these activities of government, singly or in combination, can be *the* function of government, because not all
governments perform them.

Seeking the function that all have in common, anthropologists have studied primitive groups having a minimum of government, in hopes of finding what it is that
constitutes the irreducible minimum. Lucy Mair perhaps
has carried the study of primitive government furthest
along these lines. She has examined such casual governments as those of the Nuer, who live in the southern
Sudan—"Among them certain persons are leaders in the
sense that they are respected, and people will wait to see
what they do and then follow suit"—and such minimal
governments as those of the Turkana of northern Kenya
—"The . . . belief that the very oldest men can curse
offenders . . . appears to be the only approach to
government that they have." The functional definition of
government that she offers as a result of her studies is
that, "It protects members of the political community
against lawlessness within and enemies without; and it
takes decisions on behalf of the community in matters
which concern them all, and in which they have to act
together." Yet her definition, admirable though it is in
many respects, is belied by her own studies. The Turkana
old men who curse their own tribesmen arguably may be
protecting against lawlessness within the community, but
they do nothing to protect against external enemies, nor
do they make decisions for the community. By the terms
of Lucy Mair's definition, therefore, they are not a
government, although her sound instincts impel her to

call them a government nonetheless. An all-inclusive definition continues to elude her.

Her explorations take us most of the way; but it is as far as the broadening of anthropological horizons seems to take us. The deepening of knowledge of human origins opens up other new perspectives, however, that enable us, across the broad sweep of millions of years, to go one final step further to discover what it really is that governments always do, and therefore to enable us to separate the constant element from the variables and finally come up with the answer. The work of modern ethologists and prehistorians seems to provide us with a body of relevant and applicable information—to the extent that we can accept their current findings as being at least roughly accurate. There are dangers in doing so, of course, for the prehistory we think we know is rapidly changing. The further back in time we go, the further it appears we still have to go in order to get to the bottom of things. "Very deep is the well of the past," as Thomas Mann wrote at the start of the epic *Joseph* novels; "Should we not call it bottomless?"

"Less than a decade ago the history of man was thought to have begun 600,000 years ago"—so said a scientist in 1967 at a news conference announcing the evidence which seemed to prove that man is at least 2.5 million years old. Yet even 1967 views are now out of date. The line of man's evolutionary development is now quite differently understood than it was prior to August 27, 1972, when Richard Leakey's discovery of the skull of "1470 Man" eliminated a couple of alleged ancestors of the human race. His finding extended the evolutionary time scale by two-thirds and cast doubt on theories of inherent human aggressiveness that had been based on the characteristics of apes who are no longer believed to be our ancestors.

In another connection, when the late Dr. Louis Leakey, in an expansive mood, presented evidence to support his claim that man-like creatures existed 19 million years ago, he stated that: "In terms of evolutionary history, man's separation from his closest cousins—the apes—is now carried back more than a million generations." Presumably more will be learned of these matters in the future, and undoubtedly views and conclusions will be modified and overturned. If it is arguable, however, that the human race is that far away from the point at which it split off from the apes, then theories that impute to humans the characteristics of apes require the most careful scrutiny. Presumably we could have changed a great deal in a million generations.

Yet there are family resemblances. Primates are physically vulnerable as individuals, and therefore live in groups: in other words, through natural selection, primates lacking the ability to live in groups would have died out and only those primate species inheriting the characteristic ability to live in groups survived. Primates are not a pack group and lack the innate cooperative spirit of pack-group animals. The functioning of the group is therefore only possible because of the inherited tendency to hierarchy. Hierarchical patterns (of dominance and deference) have been observed in chimpanzees, the species most closely related to humans; and this tends to support the conclusion that this propensity is an innate attribute of the species.

The propensity to government, it can be argued, therefore inheres in the genetic makeup of the human species. Granted that it operates within a wide range of variations, the disposition to behave in a hierarchical pattern seems to be hereditary. Like all dispositions and propensities, it is more highly developed in some persons than in others, and in some groups than in others. Cultural factors are of considerable importance; but the point of departure appears to be physical and genetic.

These inherited tendencies can also be seen to play a role in family life. It is not, as nineteenth-century anthropology suggested, that the government of political groups necessarily evolved from the government of the family; it is rather that, in both instances, government was generated on the basis of the same impulses. Millions of years ago the human race left the declining great forests, left the other primates behind, and learned to hunt for animals on the ground. Unable to compete as solitary hunters, the human animals hunted as a group. When the primate behavior pattern of dominance-and-deference was carried over to this first group activity, it created a rudimentary government. That was the origin of the institution.

Thus the function of government—its evolutionary function (its role, that is, in enabling the human species to survive and to progress)—can be stated with considerable precision: *it enables humans to operate as a group.* Such is its intrinsic function always and everywhere. It is what government is; it is what every government does so long as it remains a government.

The definition is perhaps best illuminated by Claude Levi-Strauss in his studies of a primitive people called the Nambikuara, who live in northwestern Mato Grosso in Brazil:

Uilikande, the native word for chief, seems to mean "the one who unites" or "the one who joins together." This etymology suggests that the native mind is fully conscious of this extremely important phenomenon which I have pointed out from the beginning, namely, that the leader appears as a cause of the group's willingness to aggregate rather than as a result of the need for a central authority felt by a group already constituted. . . .

No social structure is weaker and more fragile than the Nambikuara band. If the chief's authority appears too exacting, if he keeps too many women for himself . . . or if he does not satisfactorily solve the food problems in times of scarcity, discontent will very likely appear. Then, individuals, or families, will separate from the group and join another band believed to be better managed. . . . The day will come when the chief finds himself heading a group too small to face the problems of daily life, and to protect his women from the covetousness of other bands. In such cases, he will have no alternative but to give up his command and rally, together with his last followers, [to] a happier faction.

Why is this process not seen to occur this clearly in the civilized world? It is because we are not as free to move about as once we were. It is frequently asserted by text writers that a distinguishing characteristic of political government is that acceptance of its authority is involuntary: anyone within its area must obey it. Actually this is only true of the territorial state, and it is only significant to the extent that we are unfree to move from one country to another. Otherwise we would all be like the Nambikuara, and it would be apparent that the function of government is to create the group entity.

The United States is an illustration of this. Our large population is mainly the result of mass immigration attracted by a free and tolerant government. It is because such a government existed that the ancestors of so many Americans came in the great turn-of-the-century migrations to this country and joined the American nation. The nation was, to that extent, created by the government.

Creating a group entity is the function that defines government. All the other functions are, so to speak, optional. Among these optional functions are many of the great enterprises of the human spirit; and they seem far removed from the pedantic textbook definitions of the function of government that were previously discussed.

One of the first and clearly most important activities of humans operating as a group proved to be the development of the mind. The distinctive attribute of our intelligence is not, as we now know, the ability to make tools, for chimpanzees make tools too; nor is the large size of our brain a unique distinction, for dolphins and whales have bigger, heavier, and much more complicated brains than man, so that the pertinent question about marine mammals is now seen to be: What do dolphins and whales use their massive brains for? Since we, and not they, have achieved mastery of the world, the pertinent line of inquiry about humans should accordingly concern the direction and tendency for our thinking, rather than the size of our brain. The evidence from prehistory presented by Alexander Marshack in *The Roots of Civilization* (1972) tends to show that the human mind is uniquely "time-factored"—that is, that we think in terms of time sequence and time pattern. His evidence might be used to support a view proposed here, that the human brain, having been used for time factoring, developed as it did on that account; and the concept could be broadened along neo-Kantian lines to suggest that what is distinctively human is the extent of our intellectual ability to perceive pattern and to impose pattern. Marshack showed that the supposedly decorative markings of Neanderthal men 25,000 or 50,000 years ago were actually notation systems recording patterns in time of such occurrences as the seasons and the phases of the moon. These notations were sometimes accompanied by narrative pictures. The seasons were related to the coming of animals and of vegetation and to the swimming upstream of fish. The phases of the moon were seen in terms of death and rebirth. Eventually, close to our own time, mysterious peoples built sophisticated and amazingly precise structures to organize knowledge of the pattern of movements in the sky, the best-known monument of which is Stonehenge. These were the products of culture, and therefore of organization, and therefore of government.

To have observed the skies long enough to understand that things recur in regular patterns and then to observe long enough again to determine the nature of those patterns must have involved a group collaboration between past and present over periods of time inconceivably long to the modern world. It is sheer speculation, but might not the discipline of time observation and time patterning over hundreds of thousands of years (or millions of years, if it be that) have been the making of the distinctively human mind? How many generations must it have taken to learn that eclipses occur in cycles, when the cycles last fifty-six years?—a pattern that was only recently rediscovered at Stonehenge.

This purposeful collaborative effort involving the handing-down of information through countless generations implies coordination and group continuity, which could only have been made possible by government. Time wisdom was then a function of governmental leadership. Indeed, knowledge of the skies was an attribute of yesterday's priests and kings, and control of the calendar was an attribute of ancient government. The calendar not only listed days, but it indicated, for those who could interpret it, what happened, or might happen, or must happen on particular days. In a classical city-state, with the many duties and ceremonies of civic life, such as assemblies, rites, market days, and electoral processes, determined by the calendar, the calendar represented the life of a citizen in all of its phases. Those who controlled it could manipulate the political process. Calendar-making was not merely an essential function of the earliest known governments, but also one of its prerequisites and monopolies. The knowledge that lay behind it was a valuable, and in some cases an exclusive, asset of the government.

Closely related was the fixing of other standards,

weights, and measures, including the establishment of the precious metal content of coins. Knowledge was a province of leadership. Commerce, science, and the growth of intellectual life, invention, and technology were all made possible by the institution of government.

Government has made it possible for individuals to function as a group; and the qualitative superiority of groups to individuals has enabled the race, first, to survive, and then, in one sense of the word, to become human. Without it, there would have been no evolution of the species, no culture, and no history. On their own, our ancestors were no match for the beasts of the plain or of the forest. Yet collectively, they were able to construct astronomically-oriented monuments so awe-inspiring that men in historic times have seen in them the work of gods or of supermen from outer space.

Working collectively, human beings have had a whole world of choices available to them as to what they want to do with their lives. As with individual human beings, one of the most interesting things about groups is what they choose to adopt as their goals in life. The standard definitions of the function of government obscure the necessity for choosing such goals. By postulating that governments necessarily perform certain functions to achieve specific goals (freedom, according to Merriam; or repression, according to Lenin—to take two opposing examples), these definitions tend to remove from the open arena of debate the basic issues of political life that revolve around the central question: what *should* societies do with their collective lives? They seek to blind us to the broad range of alternatives and possibilities that are open to us—and to the need for us to choose among them.

In the twentieth century the alternatives pose themselves largely in terms of the scientific and industrial revolution of modern times. For some countries, it is a question of whether they can or should undergo the process and obtain its benefits. For others, it is a question of whether they can or should reverse the process, or in some other fashion rid themselves of its drawbacks. In considering the various issues that arise in this connection, two things, above all, should be kept in mind. The first, as has been stressed in this chapter, is that government makes it possible for individuals to become groups; and that for groups, there are all sorts of available possibilities. The second, which is the theme of the next chapter, is that even governments are limited to a very considerable extent in what they can do for the groups that they lead.

4

THE LIMITS OF GOVERNMENT

Soaring on the wings of Icarus, the modern world has dreamed that scientific technology can lift it to any heights. Not only technological problems, but social problems as well have been placed on the agenda for technological solution. Like many others, Charles Merriam termed government a technique, and it was typically modern of him to assert that it was a technique that could accomplish anything and everything.

Ancient wisdom suggests a more cautious appraisal of what can be done and a more modest notion of what should be done. Nemesis waits at the crossroads to punish pride and presumption in human beings. This is the theme and lesson of Tragedy, and, in the innocuous form of a banana peel, it is also the prop of Comedy. Tales such as those of Daedalus and of the tower of Babel caution that there is such a thing as going too high or too far. It might be well to heed the lesson that they teach.

Ecologists of the 1960s, who warned that the excesses of the industrial age would provoke the retribution of nature, may have prevented the doom that they foretold.

It is not necessarily the case, however, that such warnings will always come in sufficient time; thus a measure of forethought and self-restraint would seem the minimum prudence. The dazzling successes of modern science should not blind us to the new dangers and risks that they create, any more than we should lose sight of the new and constructive possibilities that they make available. It is marvelous that some of us can fly to the moon, but frightening that mankind as a whole may be flying too close to the sun. Thus, even if government is thought of as a technology, it would be brashly and shallowly optimistic to say that there is no limitation to what it can do. In fact, governments are not technological devices. They are neither robots, space ships, nor computers. Governments are composed of human beings; therefore they are fallible and their prospects are uncertain. They exercise a certain power, but only a limited one.

Powers and limitations are precisely what politicians are in the business of evaluating. All governments are subject to constraints which must be identified, weighed, and managed. No government is free to do exactly as it chooses. In regimes that are genuinely constitutional, there are effective legal limitations to what the government can do. Even governments that disregard the law have to take account of the practical bounds of their power. There are nuances of limitation and there are naked limitations; there are influences and there are forces. A major part of the art and practice of politics consists in determining the strength, direction, kind, durability, malleability, and number of forces in play, and then in choosing whether and how to go along with them, neutralize them, oppose them, deflect or divert them, use them, or safely disregard them in order to accomplish what we set out to do.

Politicians are occupationally prone to underestimating what can be accomplished: if they had more imagination and courage, they would be able to open up new avenues of approach. The public, on the other hand, generally tends to overestimate what can be accomplished: choices between conflicting alternatives are difficult to make, and the voters are disappointed and uncomprehending that they cannot have it several ways. Both the politicians and the public, however, understand that governments do not operate in a vacuum; the experience of practical life shows that no such academic conception corresponds to political reality.

Even the most powerful ministers of the most powerful nations feel keenly that their power to affect events falls within a narrow range. The third Marquis of Salisbury was prime minister and foreign minister of Great Britain at the height of Victorian power and glory. If anybody could have felt himself to be in charge of international events at that time, Salisbury would have been that man; yet he came to see his role as far more circumscribed. He recalled that when he was a little boy he used to think that traffic was dominated by the drivers of buses, who, in those horse-drawn days, sat on the top of their vehicles; but when he was older he came to realize that the drivers were lucky if they avoided a collision. He experienced the same realization, he said, as head of the Foreign Office.

The lack of sufficient power is an obvious limitation, but it is by no means the only one. There are intellectual limitations as well. These should not occasion any surprise, but every now and again they seem to do so. The Lyndon Johnson domestic program, especially in the area of social services and education, included ambitious initiatives that did not succeed, despite adequate funding. A considerable stir was aroused when a major research institution studied these programs and suggested that the reason they failed was that they aimed to accomplish goals nobody knew how to achieve. It is possible that these were goals we will never learn how to achieve (there are, after all, goals that are not achievable, and things that cannot be done). Alternatively, the scope of the goals may have to be changed. For example, instead of trying to improve educational and medical standards within urban ghettos, as some of Johnson's programs attempted to do, it may be necessary to go to the root of the problem and attempt to put an end to urban ghettos in order to make the other improvements possible. But can it be done?

Even if the goals can be achieved, not every government will prove capable of achieving them. Lack of skill, efficiency, and imagination often prevent the accomplishment of objectives that ought to be attained. Government officials are limited by their own lack of competence and foresight in many areas. They are also limited by the many inefficiencies and inconsistencies arising from the structure of government and society. Amongst the most formidable of these is the spectrum of distinctions and dispensations that Europe of the ancien régime described as *privilèges*. It is a term that refers to the legally recognized and legally enforceable right to receive preferential treatment with respect to taxation or other matters. Formerly, in Europe, and especially in Bourbon France, rights of this sort were sold by the government to interested private individuals. The number and variety of privileges eventually rose to grotesque proportions, and orderly administration was disrupted by the multitude of special exceptions. As a growing section of the community obtained exemptions and immunities, the whole of the national burden fell with concentrated and eventually intolerable weight upon the remaining unprivileged section. It required a revolution to reestablish the uniform application of the laws.

Privileges continue to exist in the modern world, and not merely in Europe or in other lands where the hereditary principle is engrained. They are imbedded, for example, in the detailed provisions of American tax and antitrust legislation, which extend special treatment to some but not to others. Of course, special treatment may be justified in certain cases (and each must be judged on its own specific merits), but where it becomes too widespread, the effectiveness of a government is limited: administration of the law becomes cumbersome; popular discontent is aroused by what is perceived as unjust favoritism; and the purpose of general legislation is subverted by a host of inconsistent exceptions.

To be effective, a government must be flexible and free to change policies when new circumstances so require. Privileges stand in the way of adaptability; once they are granted they are not easily withdrawn, either in law or in practice. They represent the hardening of the arteries of

society, depriving a government of the suppleness it needs
in order to succeed or even to survive.

The antidote to inconsistent government is rational,
impersonal administration of the laws by a civil service,
recruited on the basis of merit, whose practices and
procedures are published in advance and are uniformly
applied. Rational and consistent administration of this
sort is described by writers in the Max Weber tradition as
bureaucracy. As such, bureaucracy is a positive force
helping to overcome the many weaknesses and limitations of arbitrary, personal, or inconsistent government.

Bureaucracy, however, is a word with many meanings.
There is another sense in which the word is used which
describes a set of traits quite the reverse of the positive
characteristics described by Weber. Considered in its
pejorative sense as an undesirable aspect (rather than
form) of government, bureaucracy is a negative set of
qualities that limits the effectiveness of any type of
government. It is a catalogue of defects.

One of them is suggested by the very origin of the
word. The French word *bureau* is used as the term for "a
writing table" as well as for "a place in which officials
work." The word itself thus implies clerks and a world in
which paper is the chief reality. Bureaucracy in this sense
is decision making on the basis of paper work, words, and
figures, rather than on the basis of firsthand personal
inspections or face-to-face human relations. It is the
making of decisions by officials who are remote from the
realities about which the decisions are made. Objectively
this means an increased likelihood that decisions will be

wrong. Subjectively it means that the decisions, regardless of whether they are right or wrong, have a greater chance of being resented. Those who have to accept the decisions find it difficult to understand the basis upon which the decisions were made. Understandably, this makes people reluctant to support such decisions.

Closely related to these causes of bureaucratic unpopularity is the inflexible internal logic of bureaucratic practice. Issues are frequently determined on procedural grounds. Applications must be filed by certain dates, in a certain form, and in a certain number of copies. The paper work is burdensome to those who, unlike clerks, are not accustomed to it. The determination of substantive issues on strictly procedural grounds means that decisions may be based on factors that are irrelevant to the living reality. In turn this leads functionaries to forget the purpose for which they function. If the purpose is to do justice, then paper-work rules should be ignored when they interfere with the doing of justice. Government becomes bureaucratic in this sense when the broad goals of policy are lost sight of and subordinated to the procedures dictated by the internal rules of the regulators and administrators.

Bureaucracy in the pejorative sense—that is, in the sense in which it limits the effective operation of government—also refers to the characteristic inefficiencies that have come to be identified with functionaries on the government payroll: rigidity, fear of making decisions, inertia, lack of imagination, lack of initiative, and duplication of effort. Typical, above all, is the sheer quantity of unnecessary documents they produce and file away. For example, the United States General Accounting Office reported in 1973 that it cost $15 billion a year just to store and handle the government's files, many of which, says the G.A.O., are useless.

Bureaucracy means mortmain: the dead weight of that which can never be changed or removed. It means that if you elect a new government or appoint new cabinet ministers, policy will remain the same because faceless civil servants will continue to make the genuinely important decisions. It means that if you revolt, or succeed in a coup d'etat and install a new dictator, or even replace an old autocracy with a new one, again and nonetheless the same faceless rule will continue. It is an oppression not merely for what it is, but also because it seems there is no way to reject it, vote against it, dismiss it from office, or in any way get rid of it.

This ensemble of negative traits characterizes many governmental regimes. It is not exclusively or necessarily found in civil-service regimes; it can be found even in the most personal and least organized of governments. It does not constitute a distinctly modern disease; it is an ancient one as well. It limits a government in its effectiveness because it burdens society, makes people unhappy, and leads to the mismanagement of affairs and the misjudgment of situations.

A gifted generation that took its culture from turn-of-the-century Vienna and suffered from an especially bureaucratic government put these characteristics into its art and into its vision of life. A common characteristic of the Vienna school of jurisprudence, of music, and of philosophy was that in each case, once the first premise was granted, the internal logic was supposed to be pure and inexorable; there was no appeal to values outside the system. Franz Kafka wove together the strands of bureaucratically logical madness in works that made of the plight of the everyman-victim a paradigm of the human condition. The dark workings of bureaucratic government provided him with an allegory for the even less scrutable workings of destiny. An anonymous world; shadowy accusers; relentless processes having inevitable logics of their own; remote and unknown judges and decision makers; unexplained decisions; the impossibility of escape from a dooming, arbitrary, and unyielding logic: these are themes that will make Kafka's works relevant as long as human beings question the rules and justifications of the universe. As such, they will continue to keep the issue of bureaucracy relevant, for Kafka's vision transformed the terms of the discussion. He saw bureaucracy not as a mere defect displayed by certain governments, but rather as an unavoidable tragedy inherent in existence.

It is not farfetched, although it might at first appear so, that the procedures of so mundane a group as government functionaries should have given rise to speculations of this character. Governments must deal on a continuing basis with the most profound questions of philosophy, psychology, and the social sciences. In order for them to accomplish even the most ordinary and everyday tasks, their policies must take account of human nature; and few questions go deeper than the inquiry into what in fact constitutes human nature. It is a matter about which little is known with any certainty, and as such it provides one of the most complex and problematical limitations to what governments can do.

Political philosophers in the past were obliged to recognize the frankly speculative character of their theories about the nature of human beings; but for the past century or two those who have considered the matter have been able to base their views upon what science has claimed to have demonstrated authoritatively. Science, however, has not brought certainty, for what is thought to be scientific truth changes all the time. Old theories are discarded, and new ones are formulated to take their place. New facts are discovered, and old ones are found not to have been facts at all. Moreover, science does not speak with one voice; differences of opinion persist, and the inquiry continues with no more certainty than before.

Is there one human nature or many? Or is there a range within which a multitude of variable characteristics interplay? And if so, what are these characteristics? Answers to such questions are basic to political science and to an understanding of what government can and cannot do; yet the answers are not known, and they may never be known.

Evolutionists show humanity adapting and changing during the course of millions of years, but within the far shorter time span of civilization, has human nature changed and is it now changing? Is it, in any reasonable sense of the word, progressing? The lurid annals of modern political history certainly suggest grounds for skepticism. Spinoza wrote that philosophers who think they are writing political ethics are really writing satires, and that statesmen know more than philosophers because philosophers write of men as they would like them to be rather than as they are. Leibniz scoffed at projects to keep people from fighting. "I have seen something of the project of M. de St. Pierre for maintaining a perpetual peace in Europe," he wrote in a letter dated June 1712; "I am reminded of a device in a cemetery, with the words: *Pax perpetua;* for the dead do not fight any longer: but the living are of another humor . . ." It has been well and gloomily said that, "In studying the relations among governments in the twentieth century, one is struck by the realization that so little has changed since the Bronze Age."

Optimists of the Condorcet persuasion have tended to assume that if human nature *can* be changed, it will necessarily be changed in the right direction—that is, there will be a progress toward perfection. Even putting aside the matter of values (what *is* perfection?), the assumption is open to question. Indeed, much of what we are now in the process of learning about the effects of industrial society suggests that it is tending to make us into worse human beings rather than better ones, if these terms are defined in a way that would be consistent with Condorcet's general philosophy and values.

Even within an evolutionary time span, chance mutations are at least as likely to break down the genetic system as they are to enhance it. An ancient after-the-Fall view is that at the beginning of the human race there was a golden age and human nature has been going downhill ever since. In a sense Jacques Monod, who won the Nobel Prize in 1965 for biological research, offers scientific confirmation of this view. According to Monod, the life system tends to break down over a period of time, and this tendency is retarded only by the effects of natural selection, which is a form of swimming against the tide.

At the very least, Monod has shown that on scientific grounds it is arguable that changes in human nature will be for the worse. This means that the school of Condorcet can no longer assume that change will necessarily be for the better. What this further suggests is that the whole discussion ought to move on, to focus upon a consideration of the processes of change and whether and how to affect them.

Apart from human nature in general, are there certain characteristics that can be associated with particular countries? Is there, in short, a national character? That there is such a thing is, as Hans Morgenthau has said, "contested but . . . incontestable," whatever be the factors that determine and form it. It is something of which governments must obviously take account.

Human nature and national character are among the imprecisely known central realities that act as limiting factors in the domain of government and politics. There are others as well; and modern political scientists have devoted an increasing amount of attention to the delineation of what they perceive as substantive realities rather than forms and appearances. The problem is to determine what is actually real. Governments are limited both by realities and by their imperfect ability to perceive realities correctly. For politicians, no less than for philosophers, *What is real?* is therefore a basic question, the answer to which must be known in order to

understand the possibilities and limitations of governments. Is reality something permanent that lies behind
the shifts and movements of superficial appearance? Is
reality the movement? Is transition the reality? Are there
permanent interests in politics? Are there permanent
realities of geography, climate, or character that determine or influence the course of political events? Is the
relevant social reality the conflict of classes? Or is race,
rather than class, the important reality, as it was for
Gobineau? Or is nationality, which Marx ignored, the
central reality, as in the thinking of Charles de Gaulle? Is
the true political reality the inevitability and pervasive-
ness of bureaucracy in the modern world, as Max Weber
taught? Is it the inevitability of oligarchy in any society
or government? Do we in the United States today live in
Comte's reality (an industrial-technological society), in
Marx's reality (a capitalist society), in de Tocqueville's
reality (a democratic society), or in somebody else's
reality?

An understanding of what is real leads to a proper
perception of political opportunities and governmental
limitations. Thus Enver lost and Kemal won the chance
to create modern Turkey because Enver thought there
was an Ottoman Empire, while Kemal knew that only
Anatolia was politically real. Statesmen explicitly invoke
the philosophical conception to frame the terms of their
political analyses. At a meeting in 1943, when Winston
Churchill tried to allay the fears of Turkey's President
Inonu by claiming that Soviet expansion would be
prevented in the future by the United Nations organiza-

tion, Inonu replied that he wanted his country's security to be protected by "something more *real*."

What is real? Inonu thought that international guarantees were not. What of condemnations, notes of protest, embargoes, boycotts, marches, demonstrations, and other political gestures proposed by the Left and the Right: are they real, or are they rhetoric? Idealists in the nineteenth century attempted to end the African slave trade by law and by public subscription; the skeptical Marquis of Salisbury proposed instead to build a railroad to Mombasa to ruin the slave caravans and put them out of business. Was the railroad to Mombasa the road of realism? Advocates of equal civil rights for black Americans in the 1950s and 1960s proposed many measures, but Lyndon Johnson focused instead on voting rights—on the theory that voting power would bring about all the other rights. Was he correct? Is the power of the electorate the democratic reality?

What of institutions other than the state, such as the family, the church, universities, labor unions, and business corporations? Which among them are living realities? What is their actual relation to the political process? How, in other words, and to what extent do they limit national governments?

There is an ambivalent relation between the government of a state and the "government" of these other institutions. On the one hand, they are rivals for allegiance and loyalty, like kings and feudal lords locked in a perpetual Fronde. On the other hand, they offer each other mutual support. The government of the state may, therefore, be limited either by the power of such institutions, as was the emperor Henry IV when he humbled himself before Pope Gregory at the castle of Canossa, or by their powerlessness, as was President de Gaulle when a crisis in the university system nearly led to the collapse of his government.

The shifting kaleidoscope of interrelationships among government and the various powerful institutions in society is endlessly fascinating. The church has governed, as when the medieval papacy ruled its Papal States and the lamas ruled Tibet. The church has been governed by the secular authorities of the state: for example, in the England of Henry VIII. Church and state have been governed by the same individual acting in different capacities simultaneously: Archbishop Makarios, president of Cyprus and also primate of its Orthodox faith.*The deity of the church has been, as in Pharaonic Egypt, the ruler of the state. Corporations such as the East India Company have ruled as though they were governments; or like the United Fruit Company in Central America, they have overshadowed state governments; or like ITT, they have acted as a state among states; or like Litton Industries in Crete, they have proposed to undertake the functions of government on a contract basis. Still others have confused the functions of the two, like the General Tire Company, which so enmeshed itself in a Tanzanian venture that, according to a company official, they "were, in effect, part of the government and the government was part of the tire

* Makario's dual role was criticized by his opponents even before the plot to overthrow him moved forward in the summer of 1974.

factory. . . ." Today many corporations are routinely regulated by state governments; in the past, companies, such as those that established Virginia, Massachusetts, and the other English colonies in the New World, actually became state governments.

Public functions are sometimes performed and public services are sometimes provided by private corporations or business entities: these include toll roads, police and security functions, postal services, and even central banking. It is commonplace for religions and universities in the United States to become corporations. Labor unions can in large part control the government of a state, as the Histadrut does in Israel, or they can be controlled by it, as in the Soviet Union. Government of a state could be undertaken by a coalition of the "governments" of corporations, labor unions, professional associations, and other interests: such, in part, was the program of Mussolini's Corporate State. The reverse can also be done, as in state socialism, where all the other institutions of a society are ruled by representatives of the national government. In Soviet Russia the secretary-general of the Communist party controls the government; in the United States the head of government can usually control his party; and in the Arab Middle East one political party (the Ba'athists) has simultaneously controlled the governments of two different countries, Iraq and Syria.

Governments are limited by the interplay of formal structures such as these, but they also must take account of social, political, and cultural entities that are of a more informal nature than the institutions mentioned above. The nationalities question which exploded in the nineteenth and early twentieth centuries, the tribalism problem of the artificially drawn African states, and the linguistic separatisms of India illustrate the sort of issues that they raise. It is almost two centuries since the French provinces were abolished and replaced by rational *départements;* yet Brittany still claims to be an entity, and the walls of La Baule are covered with slogans demanding independence. Basques and Catalans, Kurds and Baluchis defy or deny national governments that purport to represent and rule them. There are persistent rationalizing proposals to abolish the fifty states of the United States and to regroup them into national regions. The Soviet Union has already started consolidating itself into seven new planning regions, which to some extent supersede its individual ethnic republics. But will social and political entities allow themselves to be reshaped in the interests of rational planning?

At the end of the Second World War, government leaders dealt with other countries as Solomon never seriously intended to deal with the baby: they cut them in two. The partitioned world—the world of the two Koreas, the two Vietnams, the two Palestines, the two Germanies, the two (and now three) Indias—continues to pose problems that illuminate the extent to which governments are limited by the realities of the group sense of national identity, loyalty, and hatred. Will group identity eventually conform to the partition lines drawn by statesmen and planners? Perhaps in time, it is said, for time is the unknown dimension. It may remove or it may impose limitations, but nobody knows in advance which it will do.

Largely ignored, time invalidates much political theory. Among other ways, it does so by unexpectedly affecting governmental decisions and also by limiting the effect of popular control over governments. For example, time poses particular problems for American democratic political theory with respect to foreign policy: the time lag is too long before decisions lead to consequences, and it is then too late for the electorate to reject those who made the wrong decisions.

Time is also related to the question of justice, which is found to be at the heart of classical political theory, but which is only true justice if instantly done. *Jarndyce* v. *Jarndyce*, in Dickens' *Bleak House*, is the archetype of a lawsuit that lasts so long that it consumes the lives of the parties to it. In the United States today, overcrowded trial calendars make justice to a large extent illusory. If, for example, you have a contractual right to receive x today, it may do you little good if a court enforces your right by giving you x ten years from now, when your need for x may have long since passed, when your circumstances may be substantially different, when you may be too old or too sick to enjoy x any longer, or when you may be dead.

Time also distorts the decisions governments think they make, much as wind scatters a carefully arranged pile of papers. Nobody in authority has ever seriously proposed to put into practice the "funny-money" theories of Gesell and the economic underworld of the 1930s by issuing a stamped currency that would be taxed at periodic intervals, so that people would be compelled to spend rather than save. Yet the decisions that unintentionally led to the worldwide inflation of the past decade have in effect enacted these proposals. The dynamics of time have caught up such governmental decisions in great gusts of momentum and carried them far afield.

In addition to time, there are other previously ignored dimensions that have made themselves known and felt through the unexpected crises of our age. Economic aggregates, of which governments and peoples had been largely unaware, now can be seen to express limitations of supply that constrain the functional abilities of governments. Whether or not there is enough coal or oil in the world, or whether the total food-producing capacity of the nations is adequate to fulfill national or global needs, emerge as questions of genuine importance, which make it all the more apparent that governments are limited because their resources are limited. Money, which is an expression of both resources and values, raises the question at every level of government: Are there sufficient resources to support the desired scale of governmental activity?

Are taxes high enough to meet public needs? Are they low enough to meet with public acceptance? At the intersection of those two questions falls a line of governmental limitation. In any viable society there ought to be adequate resources to support the cost of government, which is to say, the cost of authority. This includes the salaries of decision makers and the cost of police, courts, and jails, which are needed to enforce the decisions. Unless a society is exceedingly not law-abiding, these should be manageable expenses. The cost of government may rise for any one of several reasons, but the growth that generates the rise in costs should also generate the resources to pay for them. In a healthy, vigorous, and progressive society, the rising cost of government should not be a problem. The Securities Act of 1933, for example, provided that a public offer to sell corporate common stock in the United States was subject to comprehensive federal regulation. As a result of this decision, the United States incurred the expense of governing this area of activity (in the form of salaries and expenses of the Securities and Exchange Commission). Subsequent years, however, have shown this to be a good investment: the great growth in the value of American securities has not merely exceeded, but actually dwarfed the new governmental expenses involved.

The public policy questions in each new case such as this are: Do we or do we not want the federal authorities to govern a given area of activity? If so, do we want it enough so that we are willing to pay the sum of money each year necessary to do the governing? A revenue-raising alternative in almost every area is to impose the financial burden of regulation on the regulated activity by taxing the relevant transaction.

There is an exception of sorts. One way in which the cost of government grows is through population growth, which has been made possible by the benefits of industrialization. It is not until children grow to adulthood, however, that they can compensate the community by increasing its prosperity. In this connection the argument of ecologists about hidden costs assumes additional relevance. In crudely simplified form it is the argument that the growth in technological-industrial activity and population has led to pollution and depletion, which in turn have led people to realize that such hitherto unnoticed costs as waste disposal and use of resources should properly be considered as manufacturing costs and as such should be charged to the manufacturers of products. Some ecologists have gone quite far in listing the costs that have been shifted to the whole society while nobody was looking. Not even they, however, have noticed that a hidden increase in the expense of government is one of those costs.

A larger population requires, among other things, more police, more efficient police equipment, more law courts, and more jails to accomplish the same amount of law enforcement. Approached differently, what is required (according to some) is a program of political and social integration accompanied by welfare and educational programs to eliminate the supposed causes of lawbreaking. Either approach costs money. If treated as the ecologists propose to deal with hidden ecological costs (that is, to charge it to the manufacturers), the governmental cost resulting from the added population would require that an extra annual tax per child be imposed upon the parents. At the moment nobody of political consequence seriously proposes that this be done. If somebody did so, it might arouse enough shock and anger to help dramatize the contention that society must balance the economic cost against the economic value of a growing population.

All other things being equal, expanded industrial activity requires expanded governmental regulation and thus increased costs (for example, for health and safety inspections of additional industrial plants and products). New technology, too, leads to new governmental costs. New products often require testing (for example, by the Food and Drug Administration) to determine whether they are safe for public use or consumption. New areas of technology may require special regulation (for example, nuclear power by the Atomic Energy Commission). New technical developments may create additional vulnerability of society to sabotage or attack, requiring further governmental expenditures for prevention and protection. In each case those who create and sell the new technology would, in the hypothetical society imagined by ecological theorists, bear a proportionate amount of the increase it causes in governmental cost.

Real society is not what the ecologists wish it to be, much less what governmentalists would wish it to be, and so governmental costs have remained largely hidden and ignored, even at a time when ecological costs are finally beginning to be recognized. The consequences of exponential growth are only apparent at the last minute, when they are overwhelming. That has been the case with the ecological costs of the scientific-technical-industrial revolution and its attendant population growth. It has also been the case with its human and governmental costs; and these costs are now upon us without people quite realizing why.

The results can be dramatic; but they must be disentangled from the extraordinary rise in governmental expenses due to other causes. The question poses itself, for example, in terms of the reaction to New York Governor Rockefeller's initial set of proposals for cracking down on narcotics dealers. In early 1973 he proposed mandatory life sentences for convicted narcotics dealers (which would have led to an increase in the number of contested trials, because accused dealers would no longer plead guilty in return for the promise of a reduced prison sentence). What is remarkable is that opposition to the proposal by professional groups such as the Bar associations focused, not on the merits of the idea, but on the argument that there were not enough courts to try the additional contested cases, nor enough jails to house the additional life-convicts, nor enough state money to pay for the needed additional courts and jails. The proposals were open to serious objections on their own merits. Yet these objections for the most part were ignored in favor of the telling argument that the state of New York could not afford to punish the guilty. Is it not astonishing to learn that there are laws that society claims it no longer has the money to enforce? And if it is true, why and how did it happen?

If government has really become that expensive, then it tells us something ominous about the human and social costs of modern society. There is no reason why it should cost a great deal to secure respect for the law. The cost of new government should not have outstripped the growth of new resources, and it would not have done so in a socially cohesive society that was growing on an economically sound basis.

This necessarily follows from the previous discussion, in which it was asserted that the hidden cost of additional government must be figured into the calculation of whether growth in production, technology, or population is profitable or not. If the growth is truly profitable, then, by definition, it more than pays for the expenses of expanding the governmental facilities to accommodate it. Logically speaking, a case can be made for the proposition that the economic growth of modern society has been deceptive; and that, if all the true economic costs were accounted for, it would be seen that the industrial revolution has been an enterprise operating at a loss. As a practical matter, any such proposition is difficult to take seriously. It may be that we are approaching the limits of profitable economic growth, but we have not yet exceeded them. Only one other alternative remains, then, to explain why the cost of government seems to have risen disproportionately to the economic growth of the modern world. It is that a force has disturbed and disrupted the equilibrium of social processes at work in society.

The Roman Empire was discussed earlier as the outstanding historical example of a government that cost too much; and it was argued that the excessive cost of the empire was due to the lack of an ethnic foundation to give it social cohesion. The national states of the modern world do have an ethnic basis, but they have been losing their social cohesion nonetheless. It is a fundamental theme of sociological theory that the patterns of work and existence created by the industrial revolution have been the primary cause of the loss of social cohesion in modern society. This means that it is not the economic growth that pushed up the cost of government; rather, it is that the same thing that caused the growth also caused the social malady that led to the rise in cost.

The cost of government in this context, therefore, is a limitation only in a quite formal sense. It is really only a symptom or reflection of a more fundamental limitation: the absence of social cohesion. This point of major importance is frequently obscured, because people usually mean something else when they say that it costs too much to support their governments nowadays.

For the most part, when people say that government has become too expensive they mean that the social programs undertaken by the government are too expensive. These are programs that are not inherently or necessarily governmental; they would probably be undertaken privately if they were not undertaken by the public. Hospitals would be built in any event. If a government-run hospital costs a great deal of money, it is because hospitals are expensive, not because governments are expensive. The same is true of schools or of the public insurance schemes that provide social security. These do, of course, require management, whether public or private, as a component of cost; but the bulk of the money is spent for health, education, or welfare and not for governing per se (that is, for coordinating activities and telling people what to do and what not to do). The cost is primarily the cost of the activity, not the cost of its government.

There are those who oppose public programs on the grounds that it would be preferable to undertake them on a voluntary basis. They may complain about public expense, but their real objection is to the compulsory nature of government programs. Others, in the guise of an attack on government spending, are really denying the desirability of the programs for which the money is to be spent. Only those who attack government activities for being inefficient monopolies—arguing that private competitors would do the job more cheaply—genuinely raise the question of cost. The others are really debating the nature of the programs that a government ought to undertake.

In theory it is possible for a nation to undertake programs (especially military programs) too costly to be borne; and from time to time it is charged that this actually occurs. Upon close examination, however, most attacks on the level of government spending or on the level of taxation turn out to be open or disguised attacks on something else. The American Revolution began as a rebellion against taxation without representation; but while taxation furnished the occasion for the protest, it was the lack of representation that was the genuine grievance. When Louis XVI convened the States-General in order to raise new taxes, he set in motion what became the French Revolution. It did not develop, however, because the taxes he asked for were too high; it was rather that the French people objected to the nature of the regime that the taxes were going to support. The wrath of the American taxpayer is aroused every April not so much by the amount of the income tax (excessive though that be) as by the alleged inequities in the system, which is thought to allow others to escape paying their fair share.

It can be argued, rightly or not, that a lower rate of

taxation would increase prosperity and individual initiative and therefore lead eventually to greater tax revenues. This poses no objection to the level of government
spending; it is an argument about the strategy of
psychological and economic dynamics that could best
support such a level of expenditure. The process can also
be reversed, in which case it can be argued that an
increase in government expenditure—either by providing
for an improvement of the infrastructure of the economy
upon which industrial activity is based, or (following
Keynes) by taking up the slack in total demand—can
lead to an increase in prosperity that would permit a
lowering of the tax rates. These, too, are arguments about
economic strategy rather than about the upward limits of
taxation and expenditure.

A classic case against government spending is that it
deprives the individual taxpayer of his right to determine
how his money shall be spent. It has been argued that
this has already happened in the United States to a
startling extent, on the basis of the growth in government
spending as a percentage of the Gross National Product;
for the rate rose from 8.2 percent in 1929 to 22.2 percent
in 1971. The case has also been argued on the basis of the
growth of the government payroll as compared with that
of the private payroll; between 1929 and 1971 private
employment merely doubled, while government employment quadrupled.

In reply to the various arguments about government
spending, it can be said that: public needs are growing
faster than private needs; as a voter each taxpayer *is* free

to choose how the tax dollar is to be spent; and a major portion of public expenditure is used to support programs (for example, defense) that cannot be offered on an individual consumer basis, wherein only those who wanted it would buy it. None of this, however, goes to the issue of a limit on spending: it relates to the issue of the allocation of power to decide which expenditures should be made and to the issue of how society should allocate its resources. These are important issues, but they are *other* issues.

Not long ago, a journalist set out to make the argument that government spending will soon exceed the limits of the possible; and it is instructive to watch where his argument led. He began by figuring the rise in federal and local taxes from 1948 to 1972, which came to a compounded growth rate of 8 percent. With the aid of computers and technicians, he discovered that if government expenditure were to continue to rise at the current rate, total governmental expenditures by the end of the century would total $6 trillion—or, for a family with two children, $84,000 per year! Even in the face of such numbers, however, it was not really the staggering monetary totals that formed the crux of his objection to these expenditures:

All these figures may be a little mind numbing, but what really boggles the mind are the results of this spending, or lack of them. Since 1965 state and local spending has risen from $75 billion per year to $164 billion this year. Do we have better schools, better trash collection, better police or fire protection than before?

The federal government's non-defense spending, as noted

above, has grown by 144%. But are we better off now in terms of employment, slums, welfare or anything else for the fact that federal spending has more than doubled in that short time?

That, actually, is the heart of the matter: it is not so much that government programs cost too much (though they do); it is that they accomplish too little.

It is true that we ask a great deal of our government. We call upon it to make up deficiencies in the home, the school, the church, the factory, and the marketplace. We ask it to seek a national situation which is neither easy nor inexpensive to attain: a strong, stable, prosperous society that provides excellent educational and medical facilities, functioning utilities of many sorts, social securities, law, order, freedom, justice, and opportunity. We ask a lot; but we would be prepared to pay for it. Most people will go to any expense in order to live in a clean, safe community that offers excellent educational facilities for their children. Certainly taxes are too high, and they are rising at an alarming rate; nonetheless, the problem does not seem to be that people are unwilling or unable to provide the financial support for a government that could achieve their goals. The problem is rather that in our society no government seems able to achieve these goals—at any price.

There is not enough money to pay for an effective government, and governments today prove to be ineffective no matter how considerable their financial resources may be: these are two ways of describing what is really the same set of circumstances. It is a situation in which the high cost of government reflects a more fundamental defect. Governments obviously are limited by a lack of financial resources, but the financial limitation today, as in the time of imperial Rome, comes into play because of the weakness of social solidarity.

In the case of Rome, even an excellent and highly efficient government was unable to overcome this weakness. The techniques of government proved inadequate. Modern governments so far have not demonstrated that they have any greater capacity to deal with the situation. The lack of social cohesion has shown itself to be an essential limitation that can prove to be a fatal obstacle to the maintenance of effective government.

Since government techniques are insufficient by themselves to meet the needs of the situation, it is only natural to inquire whether there are other techniques that might prove more effective. Is there something that can do the thing that governments no longer can do? Is there another institution or process that might provide a promising alternative? Is there a substitute for government?

From time to time in the historical past, questions such as these have been considered with great seriousness. Now, especially in the area of international relations, the world has come back to them and to a deliberation of the underlying issues that they raise.

5

THE SEARCH FOR
AN ALTERNATIVE TO
GOVERNMENT

•

The search for an alternative to government in the
modern world is prompted by the inadequacy of national
and local governments to cope with the consequences of
the industrial revolution. In times past, such an alternative has been sought for an additional reason. It has been
sought because people have realized that all governments
are to some extent undesirable.

"Government," wrote Tom Paine in the first chapter
of *Common Sense*, "even in its best state, is but a necessary
evil." The truth of the proposition seems so evident that it
is curious that he felt the need to assert it and even more
curious that its truth should ever have been denied.
Government is a burden. It is usually expensive, often
inefficient, and sometimes ineffective. It is also fundamentally wrong, for one person should not be allowed to
rule another. Its justification is that there is no alternative. There appears to be no other technique of organizing humans into groups.

The notion that government, although an evil, is also a

necessity, does indeed seem to be the very first chapter of common sense. Nonetheless, there are some who propose a contrary theory, which is sometimes called by its proper name, anarchism, but more often is disguised under another name. According to this theory, government is as unnecessary as it is undesirable. In an assumed guise this has become an influential theory of international relations in the twentieth century; otherwise it would not deserve extended consideration, for its inherent merits are few. Anarchism is difficult to take seriously because it runs counter to all that has been learned about the nature of human beings in political society. Yet it has its advocates; apparently any political philosophy can attract at least some supporters, no matter how silly it may be and how unsilly (in other respects) they may be.

Although there are strains of anarchism in religious and idealistic thought from ancient times, it is only in the nineteenth century that the theory assumed systematic form and political shape; and it is only in the twentieth century that it began to take a significant part in world affairs, notably in the Russian Revolution and in the Spanish Civil War. It has proved a consistent failure in practice as well as in theory. Anarchism failed as a political movement even in the revolutions upon which its theorists had pinned their hopes; their principles made it difficult for them to organize even themselves.

It is not intended to suggest that anarchism is a unified, systematic, or consistent body of doctrine. On the contrary, it is a rich and varied tradition embodying diverse, and often antagonistic points of view. Some of its advocates have been pacifists, while others have preached and practiced violence. For some, anarchism was the outgrowth of a pessimistic, despairing view that only a reign of terror or a socially shattering general strike could shock people back into a sense of virtue. For others, anarchism expressed an optimistic belief that people were virtuous already. There is, however, a theme common to all anarchist thought; and that is that all people are morally good, or else that they can be made to be so by destroying the institutions that prevent people from realizing their true nature.

Many anarchist leaders were colorful and interesting personalities. The imaginative literature that they have inspired—especially Conrad's *The Secret Agent* and the novels in which Dostoevsky attempted to exorcise the demon of nihilism—is complex, fascinating, and full of subtlety. Yet their own theory is simplistic and of limited value or interest. Anarchism is a childish faith, speaking in intellectual baby talk. It postulates the essential goodness of all human beings and asserts that everyone would voluntarily act in the public interest if only there were no laws or government. Unquestionably, an opposite view of human nature underlies the institution of state organization. "But what is government itself, but the greatest of all reflections on human nature? If men were angels, no government would be necessary." So wrote the author of *The Federalist*, Paper #51, expressing no more than what everyone knows—or, rather, should know.

In effect, anarchism is the theory that all men *are* angels. It is a one-dimensional view, seeing the constructive elements but ignoring the many other traits, instincts, and forces that go to round off human nature.

It is a point of view that might be more understandable if anarchists were also quietists, that is, indifferent to worldly consequences; but in fact they have always shared a passionate concern for this world and its political fate. Even those amongst them who have followed the sinister path of criminal violence have always claimed to be acting for the social good. Their methods might have been deplorable and their objectives unrealistic, but their goal has always been to transform the existing world rather than to await the coming of the next.

The anarchist point of view can be made intelligible by casting it into millenarian form: human beings will change for the better in the distant future and *then,* after that, government will prove unnecessary. Marxists argue along these lines: men are the product of circumstances, and by changing the circumstances we can change the men. It can also be argued along lines derived from Condorcet: history is the process of human improvement, and history will continue. It can be argued on evolutionist grounds: processes of natural or artificial selection can or will produce better people. Perhaps it can be argued on other lines as well. All of these views, however, are of a hypothetical nature and to discuss them now is, at worst, pointless, and at best, premature. Yet a reasonable man could hold such views. They may be wrong, but nobody can prove them wrong, because nobody has seen the future. They are not theories that speak to our present condition; indeed, if anything, they are contradicted by the realities of contemporary existence.

At the outset anarchism locks itself into a logical

dilemma from which there is no escape. If men are by nature good, how can government be wicked, for is it not true that men invented government, or, alternatively, that it is in their nature? And is not government a group of men who by postulate are good? If government is wicked, how did it come to exist? How did one group of men come to rule another? If a group were functioning adequately without rulers, then the sudden emergence of rulers could only be explained by the presence of a wicked lust for power—but how could those who came to rule have felt this lust, given that they were primordial men, pristine and untouched by corrupting social circumstances?

According to communist anarchist doctrine, the explanation is that government arose because of private property, which it sees as a wicked commodity. But who invented private ownership of property if not human beings? If it was wicked of them to do so, they could not have been good; moreover, to say that private ownership corrupted them is to argue that the invention preceded its inventors. Anarchism is constantly being pushed to say that there must be at least some people who are bad. Once this is conceded, however, then it follows that the wicked must be controlled by the good—and so anarchism comes around to government through the back door.

Anarchists have often admitted in practice what they are unwilling to admit in theory. By acts of terrorism and by participation in the Russian Revolution and the Spanish Civil War, they too applied the methods of coercion, attempted to impose their will on other human beings, and entered into contests to determine who would govern whom—precisely the politics they had attacked.

The absurdity of it is that anarchism is a political program that must in logic prove either unnecessary or wrong. Its premise is that all men are good; but if all men are good, then there is no political problem. If all men are not good, however, then the premise is wrong; and although the problem of politics does exist, the theory, being invalid, is inapplicable to it. Thus, anarchism is a valid solution only if there is no problem. If there is a problem, it offers no solution. As Spinoza believed, a political theory that assumes the saintliness of men is superfluous.

The gentle Russian anarchist Peter Kropotkin and his idealistic colleagues relied on examples from the animal kingdom and the world of nature to validate their philosophical position. In showing that other species can cooperate on a voluntary basis, they sought to make the point that if they can do it, we can do it too. This, however, is quite untrue. Other species *are* different, and the fact that they can do these other things is often precisely part of the difference: they can do things that we cannot. What is true of them is not necessarily true of us. There are other animals besides ourselves able to function as a group, but "when the comparative animal behaviorist observes similar patterns of social behavior in two species of animals, he cannot automatically conclude that the mechanisms and processes underlying the behavior are the same for both." Other animals that are able to function as a group have physical mechanisms that make it possible for them to do so; lacking these, we have government. Thus (to use an obvious example), ant societies resemble human societies even in their division of labor; but recent studies of ant behavior show that "Practically every behavior pattern that ants exhibit is based on their responses to a limited number of tactile and chemical stimuli. . . ." Our bodies are not structured in that way, and so we do not function in that way. It is precisely because we lack a physical basis for voluntary cooperative group action that we need government as a framework in which it can take place.

This is not to say that voluntary cooperation is impossible in political society. Quite the contrary, it is not only possible but necessary; indeed, it is one of the themes of this book that such cooperation, expressing a sense of community and cohesion, is essential to the proper functioning of any government. The cooperative impulses, however, as will be seen in this chapter, are insufficient in and of themselves; they must occur in the context of central direction, coordination, and leadership supplied by the government.

In only one special, but very important, area of human political behavior has anarchist theory appeared valid and relevant to a substantial body of respectable and enlightened opinion; and that is in the area of international relations. Among the patterns of behavior that can be observed in the relations between states, there is more than one historical example of a situation in which states achieved a high level of behavioral integration with one another and in which they generally conducted their transactions (including their wars) on the basis of a comprehensive body of custom, rather than on the basis of a formal governmental structure. Europe before the

First World War is the chief historical example of such a pattern of behavior. The anarchist argument, which is usually made by people who do not realize that they are in essence proposing anarchism, is that this body of usages and customs can be developed in such a way as to fill the role of government. It is a view based on a misunderstanding of what actually happened in European history and on a confusion of two quite different things: *custom* and *law*. European history shows that even in the absence of a superior government, some states have occasionally arrived at reasonably just accommodations of their differences, and that sometimes this was done on a peaceful basis. Such observations have led some to the conclusion that all states could always arrive at just solutions peacefully. It was therefore argued that the law, order, peace, and justice, which we can achieve in our respective countries only through government, could for some reason be achieved for world society without necessarily establishing a government. If true, this would be good news indeed. But, of course, it is not true.

The error lies in the overestimation of the potential accomplishments of international law and international institutions—a potential that is actually quite modest—in such a way as to conclude that the functions of world government can be performed adequately without creating such a government. The statesmen and publicists who exaggerate the potential of international law in this way are really advocating anarchism—and they would be shocked to learn that this is what they are doing.

The issue arises in the context of the transformation of scale that has resulted from overwhelming technological and economic growth in recent times. There is no government of the industrial world as a whole, and yet decisions of a governmental character are required if that world is to continue to function. Economic growth has caused much of the world to become interconnected, and it is in the process of making the world into something resembling a unitary society. To assert that such a society can operate successfully without a government is, in effect, to propose anarchism. If anything, a society so large and complex has greater need of government than does any other.

The panic arising from the alleged oil shortage of 1973–74 has shocked many into a realization that the time has finally arrived when decisions about the allocation of scarce resources must be made for most of the earth. The multiplier effect of growing demand for goods and services on a worldwide scale has brought a whole range of commodities into short supply. There is not enough for everybody; but who is to decide how things are to be shared? The frustrations encountered in attempts by Secretary of State Henry Kissinger in early 1974 to reach agreement with the other industrial states on a common oil policy demonstrate the immense difficulty of arriving at agreed solutions for these problems on a cooperative basis.

If the allocation of temporarily scarce natural resources and food were the only problems facing international industrial society, it is conceivable that they could be dealt with on an ad hoc basis. However, there is a whole range of such problems; and they require not one-time answers, but a continuous policy. Somebody must think ahead about the future needs for capital, resources, and food, and someone must undertake programs to meet them. Somebody must organize the patterns of trade, finance, and currency to prevent the collapse of the international economy in wars of trade protectionism and competitive currency devaluations. But there is no worldwide governmental authority to do these things.

Until recently such problems of economic policy fell within the effective scope of national governments. Now that economic forces have outgrown national frontiers, it would be idle to suppose that they have been transformed in such a way that they no longer require governmental regulation. The same thing may be said about the problems of law, order, and tranquility. Traditionally national governments have preserved and enforced the peace within their boundaries, for the potential for civil violence is ruinous. Now that international warfare has also become ruinous and the maintenance of peace is required on a global scale, nothing has transformed peace into a condition that can be created in the absence of a government.

Yet there are people who assume that such a transformation has taken place. They recognize that only governments can deal with issues of this sort within national states; but they do not recognize the need for a government to deal with them when the forces, issues, and consequences grow to global scale.

As always, the shades of European international law are invoked. Repeatedly offered as an answer to the need for world order, it is as repeatedly discredited, and then offered again in refurbished form. Within its proper scope international law is an aid to civilization. As an alternative to government, however, it is a fraud.

As Sir Lewis Namier wrote at the outset of one of his historical studies, "There would be very little to say on this subject were it not for the nonsense which has been written about it." Indeed, as there has been a great deal of nonsense written about it, there is a great deal to say. There is also a great deal to say for another reason: it is important to expose the fallacy of the claim that in the domain of international relations there is a satisfactory alternative to government. Once the emptiness of such claims is made clear, energies can be concentrated on programs affording genuine promise. International law in its proper sphere has been helpful; but too often it has been lifted into another sphere and misused so as to blind people to the realities of their situation.

The anarchist distortion of international law follows from a misreading of the historical patterns of customs and usages of independent political societies. These are patterns of some complexity. Whenever independent political societies, such as tribes or nations, come into contact with one another, they find themselves in a situation not unlike the mythical states of nature described by Spinoza and Hobbes. In such a situation there is no superior governmental entity to make decisions, to define right and wrong, or to impose law; conduct, therefore, is completely unregulated. In the state of nature total freedom of behavior is circumscribed only by the force of circumstances. It is a situation which no individual human being experiences, but which every independent political society experiences. It is this important reality that gives to international relations their distinctive character; and it is the misunderstanding of this distinctive character that leads to witless and unwitting anarchism.

Three patterns can be observed in international relations with respect to standards of conduct among political societies. The first is the random pattern of arbitrary behavior in which each society does to others whatever it chooses to do, to the extent that it has the means and power to do so. When contact with other societies becomes frequent or continuous, and when dealings with other societies is believed to be advantageous, a completely random pattern of intersociety behavior becomes, and is usually seen to be, inconvenient. It impedes the orderly conduct of transactions. Thus there emerges a second pattern of behavior, which represents a modification of the first. In this second pattern of behavior, while much intersociety conduct remains random and arbitrary, certain types of transactions are conducted in conformance with predetermined standards, whether on the basis of unilateral decision, or on the basis of reciprocity (either extended or expected), or on the basis of prior (tacit or express) agreement. Among the results are such helpful practices as the granting of immunity to foreign envoys, which facilitates transactions between societies. Procedures of this sort are characteristic features of intersociety relations in many times and places, independently invented and reinvented because they are so often required by the perceived logic of the international situation. They are not, however, rules imposed upon the nations by some superior entity. By the very nature of the situation, these standards are neither enforced by nor enforceable against sovereign nations. Observance of such standards is voluntary and comes as a result either of a society's own code of propriety or of its belief that conformance to such standards are useful, convenient, or advantageous.

This second pattern is the one to which the contemporary world conforms. It is and has been the usual pattern of behavior among independent political societies. Because it is voluntary, however, as the political experience of the human race has shown, it is unwise to rely too heavily upon its taking place in any particular transaction.

A third pattern of behavior among independent political societies has arisen in special circumstances that have occurred only a few times in recorded history. It is this third pattern that has so often been misunderstood by observers and mistaken for the prototype of our own world. It is a pattern in which interstate transactions are *generally* conducted on the basis of usages and customs that are agreed upon and mutually accepted. The preconditions for the emergence of such a pattern are: first, there must be a sense of cultural unity among the politically divided societies (based often on a real or mythical political unity of the past); and second, there must be a relatively even distribution of power among the societies that leads them to take account of each other's expectations and sensibilities. An interstate system of this sort, with its attendant body of quasi-legal usage, has been dimly perceived in a number of ancient cultures—among them, the semiautonomous states of China during the first millennium B.C. The earliest model of such a system that is reasonably clear and distinct in terms of its historical outline and evidence is that of ancient Greece. The most recent and most fully developed model was that of Europe before the First World War. The situation in pre-1914 Europe is the most often misinterpreted, largely because the customs that European nations relied upon in dealing with one another at that time have persistently been described by the glamorous, seductive, inexact, confusing, and dangerously misleading phrase *international law,* about which more will be said later.

Basically any system such as that of classical Greece or of modern Europe expresses a sense of group exclusiveness: "There was a recognition of certain rules and customs as between peoples of cognate race; the obligation to observe them in regard to those outside the pale was either not admitted or much less stringent." In Greece as elsewhere, this obligation was at first conceived in a religious context. Treaties were supposed to be kept because they were witnessed by the gods; and it followed that obligations were limited to those who worshipped either common gods or gods who were on friendly terms with the gods of the group. The Greek city-states developed "a body of Hellenic public law which merited the name of international law as much as, say, modern European law merits it." Phrases used by the Greeks to describe their interstate customs included "the common laws of the Hellenes." These customs expressed a unity against the alien world; foreign states were not dealt with on the basis of them.

European public law, like that of ancient Greece, developed in the context of a common religion. As an additional background it had the shared experience of Roman imperial rule. After the collapse of Rome, relations among the temporal powers of Europe continued to be thought of in terms of Roman law and in terms of the Catholic faith. When Isidore of Seville wrote in the seventh century about the laws of war and peace and truces and treaties, he dealt with essentially the same sort of subject matter in the same sort of way that international lawyers of a later date have done. His account, unlike theirs, however, was coherent, for he wrote in the context of a Europe that still considered itself a Roman unity and that was in fact a Christian unity. The customs of interstate behavior, as they emerged in medieval Europe, were the internal rules of Christendom. They were politically real because the papacy was politically real.

The challenge to the moral authority of these customs came when Europe encountered the New World. The Spanish precursors of international law, Vittoria and Suárez, expounded the rules of inter-Christian state behavior and knew that they were not applicable to the Indians of America, to whom nothing was owed; but Vittoria took pity on the vulnerable Indians and tried to develop a doctrine that would protect them from unbridled bad faith and savagery.

The problem came next to Europe itself with the

Reformation. When Europe had two religions rather than one, would the practice of keeping treaties and observing the accepted customs apply only, on one side, among Catholic states, and, on the other side, among Protestant states? On the contrary, the unity of European culture overcame the division of European religion. Once, after the bloodbath of the Thirty Years' War, and again, after the French Revolution and the Napoleonic Wars, the European nations developed interstate customs of behavior that were generally observed, regardless of religious differences, in their behavior with one another, although not in their behavior toward most others. The ambit of these customs eventually expanded to include states of European ethnic origin and a few exceptional others.

The basic assumption and the most telling characteristic of this set of customs was the sovereignty of national states. From it all else in fact and necessarily followed. *Sovereignty* is used here in its essentially political sense relevant to the problems of war and peace; and it is used to mean the authority that can, in the last resort, make the decisions. In relations among states, sovereignty means independence; and the European states were in fact independent and could exercise such independence as far as their relative power permitted; that is, the independence of one ended only where the independence of another began.

The flow of custom was horizontal rather than vertical; it was something between entities, and not something imposed upon them. Each nation made its own decisions about the substantive content of the customs it would follow; each made its own decision about which other nations it would observe those customs with; and each had to avenge its own injuries if it did not receive at least the customary courtesies from other nations.

The customs were followed only when the issues involved were not of vital importance, for, although standard textbooks assert otherwise, the customs were not binding. What this means is that even in the event a national government did not behave according to the minimum standards expected of a civilized European nation, the population of that country would nonetheless continue to follow the leadership of its government. Then as now, national governments were politically free to move as they chose, regardless of customary rules. They made the ultimate decisions: they might or might not observe the customs, and their respective countries would support them no matter which course they chose. By way of contrast, at various times during the Middle Ages princes were bound (that is, kept from freely moving) by the law of Christendom as interpreted by the pope, because in case of conflict the people would obey the pope rather than the local ruler. Thus the local rulers were not politically free to move as they chose; they were restrained and constrained to act within the ambit of the rules.

In the emerging modern Europe, on the contrary, states were not bound by any rules of international conduct. There was no authority higher than the various national governments, and so irreconcilable conflicts between them—conflicts about things people felt to be important—could be decided only by warfare. Wars were limited in scope and in aim; they were the duels of professional armies and interfered little with civilians, commerce, or neutral countries. They were "temperate and indecisive contests," as Gibbon wrote in their praise.

The customs governing international relations were morally neutral. By definition, they were the way people actually behaved, rather than the way that anyone thought people ought to behave. Facts were accepted: if a nation conquered a territory and its adversary conceded the loss, then the territory belonged to the conqueror. The most recent peace treaty defined the accepted rules until a new war took place; then a new peace treaty would define new rules. There was no normative content: the law simply went with the winner.

The European balance of power made the system workable. No country was powerful enough to disregard the views and sensibilities of its neighbors. The courtesies and civilities of international usage were enforced by a knowledge that a failure to behave properly might arouse hostilities that could tilt a delicate balance in an unfavorable direction.

The actual rules embodied in the customary behavior of European states toward one another were, for the most part, the rules of Roman law. The customs developed and were observed because Europe was an entity of social, cultural, and religious unity, which attracted a measure of genuine group loyalty. There was also the historical unity of Rome, the papacy, feudalism, and the empire founded by Charlemagne and Otto the Great. Voltaire and Gibbon wrote of Europe as though it were one republic, divided into several states, but observing the same conventions and principles. The Europeans had common classics, common educational formations and experiences, common values and views, and a common level of technology. The texture of allegiance was strongly horizontal: dynasties and aristocracies even of rival countries were related by blood or marriage; guilds were of transnational scope; the clergy owed loyalty to pan-European organizations; and there were statesmen (Talleyrand is the supreme example) who, in case of a conflict of loyalties, chose to serve the welfare of Europe rather than the narrow welfare of their own country.

Then came the First World War, and things changed. Europe had been superseded, as A. J. P. Taylor observed: "what had been the center of the world became merely 'the European question.'" The political world that emerged from the war had broadened to include the entire globe. Formerly all of the great powers had been heirs to the European tradition and a part of its culture; all had partaken of its customs. This was no longer true. The political world of the twentieth century came to be dominated by powers who did not share values, history, religion, or ideology, and who had no shared customs of interstate behavior.

No doubt there was a great deal wrong with the way in which Europe governed her own affairs, and those of most of the rest of the world, before 1914. Yet there were virtues, too, and many of them have disappeared from the political world of the twentieth century. Among these were the traditions of courtesy and respect that expressed themselves in the customs of international law. Fundamental changes in the political structure of the world were certainly required; but, in retrospect, it is not clear that all of the important changes that occurred as consequences of the First World War were the right ones.

In terms of the structure of governmental institutions, it can well be argued that 1914 was the year in which history turned in the wrong direction. Alexander Solzhenitsyn has interpreted Russian history in this sense, pointing to the First World War as the beginning of a false turn by his country toward an alien system of government. The transformation of what was before 1914 a conservative imperial Germany into a Nazi state was so wrong a change that Thomas Mann in his novel *Doctor Faustus* portrayed it as a pact with the devil, perhaps leading to eternal damnation. In less dramatic terms, Secretary of State Kissinger, in widely quoted, informal remarks reported in early 1974, suggested that ever since the outbreak of war in 1914, the various European governments have been, to a considerable extent, without legitimacy. His reference apparently was to a concept developed by one of his fellow historians of the Congress of Vienna, according to which governments are legitimate only when there is full mutual confidence between the government and the governed. Undeniably the First World War broke up the general structure of politics and society in which such confidence had previously reposed; few European governments can now obtain from their populations a general acceptance of their conduct of national affairs. Thus there is considerable validity to Secretary Kissinger's observation.*

* A critical European might well retort that, as a result of the

Not merely in the structure of government, but also in the structure of the relationship between governments, fundamental changes of an unfavorable character were among the consequences of the First World War. Previously there had been a balance of power that restrained individual governments, and there also had been a shared culture that inhibited excesses. The breakdown of the old order inaugurated a century that has been characterized by disequilibrium, lack of restraint, and the growth of political and technological forces that seemingly know no bounds to their advances, no matter what stands in the way.

Woodrow Wilson and the other leaders of the Allied powers that won the First World War succeeded in changing the structure of the political world; but they did not foresee all of the consequences of their doing so. They expressed an intention to give national self-determination to the peoples of the world; and they did indeed succeed in initiating the process by which this important goal was eventually won for most of the world. Wilson had also intended to expand the role of international law in world affairs, but here he failed because he misunderstood the nature of that role and its inherent limitations. His program aimed at the destruction of the European balance of power, which he viewed as a manifestation of national selfishness. He did not understand that the central mechanism of the European polity, the balance of power, was closely interwoven with the civilized customs

---

Vietnam War, the government of the United States has also lost its legitimacy in this sense.

of behavior previously found among the European states. Wilson proposed to expand those customs by destroying the very mechanism that made them possible, but which therefore defined the limit of their capability. As Immanuel Kant wrote in the Introduction to *A Critique of Pure Reason*: "The light dove, cleaving the air in its free flight, and feeling its resistance, might imagine that its flight would be still easier in empty space."

In the Wilsonian tradition of idealistic internationalism, the overthrow of the old European order in the First World War was thought to have ushered in an era of greater world harmony based upon an expanded international law and upon new international institutions. It was said that international law now applied to the whole community of nations, rather than merely to those of Europe, and that to an increasing extent it now governed major areas of international relations. The evidence of half a century, however, now tends to belie such claims. These have been the bloodiest years in the history of the world. Never have the customs of civilization been so horribly violated as in such deeds as the massacre of millions of unarmed and helpless European Jews. Nor was this an isolated episode. Bloodthirstiness has become endemic. In the twentieth century it has become normal to launch undeclared wars, to bomb civilians, and to employ weapons of mass destruction. In such important areas as the protection of civilians and the mitigation of international conflict, international law seems to be playing a lesser role in actual events than it did in the days of the European system, rather than a greater role, as claimed by proponents of the new international law.

In these respects history took another wrong turning in 1914. The Wilsonian school of thought failed to understand or to appreciate the full merits of the restraint and moderation characteristic of the old order in Europe that they rejoiced in overthrowing.

Understanding the complex pattern of interstate customs formerly observed in Europe would have been difficult in any event; it was made almost impossible by the habit of describing the pattern as international law (a phrase suggested by Jeremy Bentham). It was in some respects a valid description, but it impeded rather than facilitated an exact understanding of its subject matter. Its subject, true enough, was a body of customary rules that were observed among nations; but only among *some* nations, not among all. To provide a better description, Bentham should have coined a word like *inter-some-nation-al*. Moreover, he should have found a better word to describe the body of rules themselves. While it was not invalid to use the word *law* in this context, it was unhelpful to do so. True, the usage could be described as law in a couple of senses: custom is by rhetorical analogy called law (as, for example, in the phrase "the laws of hospitality"); and descriptive generalizations are also referred to as law (as in "the laws of group behavior"). It was not law, however, in the ordinary sense in which we use the word (as when describing arson or homicide as "against the law"). Yet it is precisely *law* in this sense of the word for which the modern world has been searching. The Benthamite phrase has become a mirage for those who want to believe that we have arrived at the oasis before we have actually done so.

The term *international law* always has been a morass of semantic confusion. Discussion of the subject is constantly bedeviled by the misleading use of it in such a way as to arouse false hopes and expectations. Most texts and treatises begin by pointing out that they employ the word *law* in a special sense; nonetheless many then go on to use the word in its ordinary sense. Lawyers have been especially bad about this; they mislead by formulating the subject as though it were their own. Diplomatic historians have been better; but anthropologists could have been better still, for the description and analysis of group customs is their special skill.

Perhaps the most accurate description of the subject was that once supplied by Hans Morgenthau. More than three decades ago, he wrote a deservedly famous essay, "Positivism, Functionalism and International Law," upon which, surprisingly, neither he nor anyone else has ever really elaborated. In it he argued that international law was a reflection of reality rather than a reality itself. Like the moon, it shown with a light that was not its own. As he pointed out, municipal law provides a mechanism for changing behavior and is a cause of changes in behavior. European international law, on the other hand, was not a cause, but a result; it was not a force, but the reflection of the interplay of forces; it was a cultural manifestation and function of a particular historical episode in modern Europe. For nearly three centuries the independent nations of Europe behaved among themselves in an especially civilized way because of a unique combination of political, economic, historical, religious, and cultural factors. The only way to alter the system was to change those underlying factors.

The focus of relevant discussion in the twentieth century has been on the mechanisms that can effect a change in conditions, because a radical change in international behavior increasingly is perceived as a prerequisite to the well-being, and perhaps to the survival, of the human race. The world as a whole is now seen to require domestic peace, the administration of justice, and the prudent management of its economy, its environment, and its resources. These are the tasks of government; but in the absence of a world government, the search for an alternative to government has centered on the possibilities afforded by international law and institutions. Earlier in the chapter the belief that such possibilities do exist was termed a species of anarchism, because it asserts that tasks that only a government can fulfill within a national state can be fulfilled on a worldwide scale by some process or institution other than government. There is no historical precedent to support such a claim. The tasks set forth today are tasks that international law did not perform in the European world order that prevailed before 1914. Proponents of a changed and expanded international law as a solution to the world's new problems have failed to come to grips with the problem of how changes in international behavior can be effected so as to solve the new problems. Within a sovereign nation the behavior of its subjects can be changed by legislating and enforcing a change in the law. No such method of effecting change is available to the world community, however, because there are no subjects: the various nations of the world are independent of one another. Those who propose international law as a solution to the problems of the twentieth century have not perceived this distinction; and their failure to do so is a consequence of their using *law* in the usual and ordinary sense, after having defined it in a different and special sense. They have dealt with the problem of trying to make changes in international behavior as though they were working within the framework of a properly constituted and operative legal system; theirs has been a program that has consisted of negotiating and executing legal documents. In the context of a world without law or government, and in the face of violent and uncontrolled global forces, it is a program that often has shown itself to be both futile and superficial.

The first new public need to be perceived widely as a consequence of the First World War was the necessity for permanently preventing international warfare; it was recognized that the technology of destruction had grown to a point where it was out of hand and could endanger the survival of the species. Clearly a profound transformation of human political behavior would be required in order to guarantee perpetual peace among independent and sovereign entities. The method adopted to effect such a transformation was the Kellogg-Briand Pact (1929), a multilateral treaty renouncing the use of war as an instrument of national policy. According to the literature of the new international law, aggressive warfare thereafter became an international crime; but nations have continued to go to war with one another nonetheless. As a method of changing international behavior, the treaty proved to be ineffective: to call aggressive warfare a crime accomplished nothing in the absence of a global government to prevent and to punish crimes.

The experience of the United States with its network of similar peace-keeping treaties in the earlier part of the century seemed, similarly, to demonstrate their pointlessness. George Kennan has described the American governmental experience with these documents in the following way:

The United States Government, during the period from the turn of the century to the 1930's, signed and ratified a total of ninety-seven international agreements dealing with arbitration or conciliation, and negotiated a number of others which, for one reason or another, never took effect. Of the ninety-seven, seven were multilateral ones; the remainder, bilateral. The time, trouble, and correspondence that went into the negotiation of this great body of contractual material was stupendous. Yet so far as I can ascertain, only two of these treaties or conventions were ever invoked in any way. Only two disputes were actually arbitrated on the basis of any of these instruments; and there is no reason to suppose that these disputes would not have been arbitrated anyway, on the basis of special agreements, had the general treaties not existed. The other ninety-five treaties, including incidentally every single one negotiated by Secretaries of State Bryan, Kellogg and Stimson, appear to have remained wholly barren of any practical result. Nor is there any evidence that this ant-like labor had the faintest effect on the development of the terrible wars and upheavals by which the first half of this century was marked.

Some proponents of the policy of achieving peace by the negotiation of treaties believe themselves to have been vindicated by the action of the war crime tribunals at Nuremberg after the Second World War. There are those to whom the Nuremberg judgments seemed to represent a transformation of the new international law into a functioning system capable of enforcing justice. Yet no change in the basic realities had been wrought. At Nuremberg it proved possible to execute the captured leaders of the defeated nations; but that had always been possible, with or without a legal system. The transformation that law effects in human affairs is that it makes it possible to secure justice from the powerful and not merely from the weak. The Nuremberg trials would have marked a genuine change in world affairs only if they had resulted in the execution of the victors rather than of the vanquished. Whatever may have been their merits, the Nuremberg judgments changed nothing; they left the real world where they found it. Confirmation of this was provided by subsequent events. The Soviet leaders were not placed on trial as a result of their invasion of Hungary in 1956 or of Czechoslovakia in 1967. Those responsible for the Korean and Indochinese wars have not been placed on trial. Middle-Eastern wars between Israel and her neighbors have raged for a quarter of a century, but no trials have taken place. The new international law has not succeeded in changing the world.

The need for change is there, however. The world now requires not only peace, but also the administration of its economic and environmental affairs. The dismal record of international law in attempting to prevent warfare in the twentieth century demonstrates its incapacity to effect fundamental changes in the political world. It was inappropriate to employ it in this endeavor, to which it has never been suited.

It should have been clear from the outset that only governmental techniques could effect the necessary changes, and that techniques relying merely on voluntary cooperation would prove inadequate. Such has been the universal political experience in achieving similar goals of domestic peace and economic regulation at the local and national levels. In part, as has already been noted, the weakness in the program of offering international cooperation as an alternative to government was disguised by employing a special concept of law in a misleading way, one that hid the relevant difference between customs and laws. The attempt to place international cooperation on an organized basis by creating institutions such as the League of Nations and the United Nations was also made to appear in an excessively favorable light by yet another confusion of concepts. Much of the hazy thinking about these international institutions has resulted from a failure to observe the distinction between a diplomatic *conference* and a *congress*.

A congress is a body that makes decisions for a group that constitutes a unitary entity. A conference, on the other hand, is an assemblage of the representatives of individual decision makers; it convenes for the purpose of reaching agreement through negotiation and compromise. The final decisions reached by a congress are collective decisions; in a conference they are individual decisions, that at best are reached on a mutual basis.

The confusion of the two terms has historic roots. The international peace conference was a distinctive diplomatic development of the fifteenth century, when European Christendom was still a real entity and the rulers who assembled at the conference could reasonably be considered a collective body. The fifteenth-century Congress of Arras has been called the first great international peace conference. Its most recent historian tells us that "it should be treated as one incident in the long history of papal mediation between the states of Europe," and that the ecclesiastical aspect of the treaty made it difficult in a religious age to avoid compliance with its terms. Thus, like European and classical international law, the international conference in its origins owed its efficacy to religious sanctions.

Later international peace conferences, such as those of Westphalia (1648) and Utrecht (1713–15) moved further and further from the ambit of religion into the sphere of secular politics, where each ruler was sovereign, independent, and free to make individual decisions. In modern revolutionary Europe the first great international peace conference was the Congress of Vienna (1814–15). The enormous influence of this conference is woven through the texture of nineteenth- and twentieth-century politics and continues to affect us significantly today. Sir Charles Webster prepared his monograph *The Congress of Vienna* at the request of the librarian of the Foreign Office for use at the Versailles peace conference (1919); and, later, he served as the leading British expert at the San Francisco conference (1945) to draft the United Nations Charter. Sir Charles and his great friend and rival H. W. V. Temperley carried over their scholarly debate about the Congress of Vienna into the international politics of the twentieth century, in which they were both active. The most recent major historian of the Congress of Vienna, Henry A. Kissinger, has carried on this tradition of applying an interpretation of what happened at Vienna to the problems and opportunities of international life in the twentieth century.

The allies against Napoleon, like the allies against the Kaiser and the allies against Hitler in our own century, imagined that their negative wartime unity of purpose would carry over into the postwar world. They thought in terms of an organization that would have the nature of a permanent alliance, making and enforcing collective decisions. This proved to be an unreal vision.

Central to the drama at Vienna was the deliberate confusion of the concepts *conference* and *congress*. The term *great powers* entered the diplomatic vocabulary in 1814, and the distinction between them and the small powers became formal. Whereas the deceived small powers thought that they were to attend a *congress* in which all might participate, there was in fact a *conference,* at which the decisions were made by an inner group consisting of the great powers. Talleyrand, in deft maneuvers, brilliantly exploited the pretensions implicit in the concept of a congress. He began by posing as a spokesman for the excluded smaller powers and then allowed himself to be bought off by admission to membership in the governing eight. The eight then postponed the plenary sessions of the congress indefinitely. "In fact," as Friedrich von Gentz, secretary general of the congress, subsequently remarked, "there never was a Congress of Vienna."

The confusion of the concept continues. On the one hand, there is the realistic understanding that peaceful programs can be adopted only if the great powers are able to reach agreement. To achieve goals along these lines there exists today the useful format of an international conference, that is, the Security Council concept of the United Nations. On the other hand, there is the unrealistic concept of a congress, as manifested in the General Assembly concept (wherein Upper Volta and the United States have the same importance in that they each have one vote) and in the misleading, pretentious name "United Nations." The name suggests an entity, which is a deception, for there is nothing there but representatives of the various governments and their employees.

The League of Nations was also an extension of the congress concept and, as such, it too expressed the anarchist approach. The League was based on the unanimity principle and was nonetheless supposed to solve international conflicts peacefully. If all participating governments were in agreement (in which case, of course, there was no need for it), the League could "work," but if there was disagreement or conflict, it could not work. The anarchist fallacy also characterizes the concept of the United Nations as the preserver of world peace. When the great powers are in conflict, the United Nations is really nothing more than the umbrella that folds in the rain, for it can only act if the great powers are in agreement. The usefulness of the United Nations lies only in its Vienna-Eight or Security Council aspect as a permanent diplomatic conference at which agreements can be reached easily because conversation and contact are always taking place.

Like the international law it represents, the permanent diplomatic conference of the United Nations works through techniques of voluntary cooperation, accommodation, and compromise. Therefore it is inadequate to meet the new demands and needs that have arisen in the twentieth century for an agency to fill the role of a government on a worldwide scale. Its failure to bring peace and justice to the world was demonstrated by its helplessness in the face of Soviet action against Hungary in 1956 and Czechoslovakia in 1967, its inability to deal with the problem of United States involvement in Vietnam, and its failure for more than twenty-five years to resolve the armed conflicts between Israelis and Arabs. Even Richard Gardner, a leading proponent of the United Nations who has always written about it in a sympathetic and constructive spirit, has recently stated that, "If a clear and unambiguous case of aggression came before the Security Council or General Assembly today, there would be little confidence that a majority of members would treat it as such or come to the aid of the victim." The United Nations has failed to keep the peace. It has not provided a genuine alternative to world government, for it has not done the important things that governments can do. The continuing problem of the modern world has been that such things therefore remain undone. For more than half a century, the world has searched for an alternative to world government, but has not found it.

Ever since the First World War, it has been increasingly clear that a world society is in the process of emerging. Like any other society, as it fully emerges it requires a government if it is to continue to function effectively. World forces of production and of destruction have upset the patterns of existence because there is no world government to deal with them; nor is there any immediate likelihood that such a government will be created. Voluntary cooperation among the nations is insufficient and affords no prospect of a unified approach. The European international law that flourished before 1914 was incapable of dealing with important interests of this sort. Today we are perhaps even farther from being able to do so, for since the end of the First World War, the powerful nations of the earth have not abided by the ties of comity that alone made possible even so limited a body of comprehensive international custom as European international law.

In the short run there is no alternative but to deal with the situation as it is; and this requires aiming at solutions that are based on self-interest and that are self-enforcing. In seeking to curb the international arms race, for example, no reliance can be placed on the general desire of governments to avoid ruinous warfare, for since at least 546 B.C., when representatives of fourteen Chinese states met to secure perpetual peace by general disarmament, the program of achieving peace through disarmament has proven to be a failure. A proliferation of disarmament and arms-control treaties in the contemporary world has had similarly little effect. Since the end of the Second World War, despite the multitude of new treaties, the cost of armaments throughout the world has increased at a rate greater than that of population or of gross national products. The cause of the failure seems to be reasonably clear. As Hans Morgenthau has written, "Men do not fight because they have arms. They have arms because they deem it necessary to fight." Any realistic attempt to limit the arms race must take account of the desire to expand national military power. A countervailing national desire, however, is now provided by the increasingly overwhelming cost of modern weapons. This makes it possible to envisage the success of certain types of negotiated programs of restraint, such as the strategic arms limitation talks currently being conducted by the United States and the Soviet Union. Modern techniques of monitoring and aerial inspection seem to provide assurance that the restrictions that are agreed upon will be observed in practice, for fear of reprisal; but it is always conceivable that newer technologies will invalidate the process by making it possible to counter the present techniques of observation and control. Thus the self-enforcing aspect of these arrangements may be somewhat fragile; and, if so, new approaches will have to be found.

Ad hoc international accommodations of this sort are made possible only by the perception of mutual or common interests. As the problems of the world grow to be more dramatic and severe, it might be hoped that the recognition of such interests would occur more frequently and that further breakthroughs to international cooperation might take place. Yet the oil crisis of 1973–74 and the continuing crisis of the world monetary system demonstrate a persistent blindness to the community of interests and to the benefits of international cooperation; they also show that national governments will not give up their short-sighted, selfish policies even for the sake of avoiding financial ruin. Only the threat of physical destruction seems sufficient to forge the bonds of unity; indeed, wartime alliances are the only ones that seem almost always to work—for the duration of the war.

International cooperation based upon the perception of mutual or common interests therefore affords little scope for common action, even though it is the only basis for general cooperation that now exists. One conclusion to be drawn is that, in the pursuit of constructive policies, governments will have to work within many overlapping international groupings; on any given issue, only a limited number of nations will be able to see that there is a community of interests, and those may well be different nations in each case, depending upon the issue. Another conclusion to be drawn is that efforts should be made over the long run to transform the basis of international cooperation and to raise it initially at least to the level of comity prevailing in Europe before 1914, if that can be done.

International law and institutions can play a modest but constructive role in attempting to achieve such an objective. A positive program along these lines might proceed as follows:

1. Continue the excellent work of codification and agreement with respect to the rules that should govern international transactions (for example, the treaty on treaty law);

2. Concentrate attention and effort on areas where important state interests are not in conflict (in other words, areas where customs and treaties will do some good, because they will be observed);

3. Describe the customary rules not merely in general terms, but in terms of particular points of view (as Charles Hyde did of international law according to the United States; as H. A. Smith did with respect to Britain; and as Georg Schwarzenberger did with respect to international tribunals);

4. Following an inspired suggestion by Roger Fisher and Richard Falk, attempt to raise the level of international conduct by incorporating more international law into the municipal law and bureaucratic norms of the various states, thus making use of the actual structures of power and loyalty that exist in the world today;

5. Change the nomenclature to eliminate pretentious and misleading terminology such as "international law";

6. Do not expect compliance with treaties or customs where compliance would run counter to perceived state interests that are believed to be of importance;

7. Make an especial effort to restore the courtesies that formerly characterized international dealings;

8. Reform international organizations so as to reflect their true character and purpose.

This latter should particularly be done with respect to the United Nations, which has aroused too many exaggerated expectations and has performed inadequately even in terms of that which it could be expected to accomplish. A positive program to improve the United

Nations could well begin by changing its name to something that accurately describes it, such as "the Permanent International Conference." Shams and name calling should be eliminated as unhelpful; there should be no more futile public debates, no more meaningless voting, and no more resolutions and condemnations. Verbal disputes in which the Arabs and their friends vote that the Arabs are marvelous and the Israelis are terrible, while Israel and her friends vote the opposite, are no more than cheers for the home team and boos for the visitors—all of which do nothing to help the cause of world peace, but do a great deal to put everyone in a poor temper for conciliatory talks. Emphasis should be placed instead on the positive contribution that can be made by the continuing development of a world agora, conducive to quiet and patient diplomacy, where agreements can be reached and compromises achieved. Horizons should be broadened. Not merely the Big Five of the Security Council, but all of the advanced industrial powers must group together to undertake joint endeavors for the common good. This must not be done in competition with the United Nations; it must be a complementary effort, or else the grouping of the Big Five should be opened up and expanded. Cooperation need not be on a structured basis, nor need it include all of the powers when not all of their interests are concerned. The emphasis should be placed on practical accomplishment rather than on formal procedure.

No useful purpose is to be served, however, by pretending that international groupings—any more than the development of international civilities, usages, and customs—can adequately perform the range of functions that governments perform for domestic society. The exaggerated claims made for them by an anarchist philosophy lead to widespread disillusionment when the lack of results becomes evident. This, in turn, detracts from the real and useful purposes that international law and international organization can perform in the modern world.

This is not to say that world society does not *need* the performance of governmental functions, even as domestic society does; far from it. There are global needs, global opportunities, and global responsibilities, all of which require a world government. Yet there is neither world government nor a sense of world community, which alone could sustain such a government.

In the long run the solution must be a strategy to achieve the world community that does not exist today. Hans Morgenthau and David Mitrany have persuasively advanced a strategy based on patient diplomacy, a lessening of tensions, and the development of functional integration. Such an approach would not merely solve particular problems on a supranational basis; it would also aim at generating a widening of loyalties that would rise above the narrow confines of nationalism. To do all of this, however—if it can be done—will take time.

In the years it would require to undertake such a program and then to bring it to completion, the structure of world order is likely to be tested by strains more severe than it has ever known before. Ever since the end of the Second World War, the world has existed in the shadow of fearful military insecurity. That continues to be the case. In addition, the world economy has now entered into a phase of dangerous uncertainty as well. At best, the interconnecting system of trade, production, and finance in the modern global economy is an intricate and fragile structure. No one can say with great assurance that it will survive the onset of forces that started in motion long ago, but have become apparent only in recent months and years. The oil panic of 1973–74 and the parallel run on short supplies of food and other commodities highlighted a shift in power and resources within the structure of the industrial revolution. Whether the change proves to be temporary or permanent, it is nonetheless of a fundamental character. Formerly the relatively few manufacturing countries exercised power in a world of abundant natural resources. Now manufacturing facilities are widespread, while natural resources are becoming scarce; and the suppliers of natural resources have asserted a claim in effect to replace the resource-poor manufacturing countries among the holders of the world's wealth and power. Meanwhile a third group of nations, lacking both industrial and natural resources, has already been impoverished by the lack of one and now is doubly doomed and impoverished by the lack of the other.

Is it possible that demands for so massive a transfer of wealth and power will be, on the one hand, peacefully granted, or, on the other, voluntarily moderated? Is it likely that nations in the third group will resign themselves to perpetual poverty, or that wealthy nations will volunteer to share their riches with them instead? It would be difficult enough to regulate and adjust to the

shift of resources and power and the competing demands
if there were a government in place to do so. Diplomatic
conferences are no adequate substitute for government,
and their limited resources will be sorely tried. Encour-
agement may be taken from the fact that so many
negotiations are now in progress to deal with international matters of this sort, and that leaders of opinion in
such large numbers have been asserting the need for
achieving international collaboration in these spheres.
However, remembering how difficult it is to obtain unity
of action even when international interests are similar,
the problems that arise in trying to reach international
understanding when interests are in conflict should not
be underestimated.

It is in these economically and politically hazardous
years ahead that the world must also meet the challenge
of trying to forge a common civilization for itself, or for
such parts of it as prove ideologically amenable to a
program of unification. The aim is to create a community at least as unified as that of Europe before 1914.
Such a unity would express itself in similar customs of
international behavior, characterized by moderation and
restraint in the pursuit of national goals. Yet the world
could not rest there, for international customs do not
provide an adequate alternative to government. Like
contemporary Europe, the world would be obliged to try
to go forward to a higher political form rather than back
to 1914. In both cases the endeavor is an uncertain
enterprise. The reality of the community in both cases is
basic to the possibility of success. The Common Market,
which is in process of strain and evolution today, was

originally a program expressing an ancient vision of Roman and Christian unity stretching back two thousand years. As such it was the shared dream of Adenauer, Schuman, and de Gasperi—three old men who were heirs of that tradition and whose cultural roots were nourished by its soil. Opponents of unification, who think of Europe as a merely geographical notion, fall back on Bismarck's brutal sarcasm, *"Who is Europe?"* Other opponents of the unifying concept more gently suggest that though the European community may once have existed, its basis was religious: in a secular world it has disappeared along with the faith that inspired it. In this vein André Malraux recently remarked that "there was a Europe because there was Christianity. Christianity was serious. Europe is a dream. . . ."

Similarly, questions will be asked about the reality of the world community, assuming that sufficient progress takes place to make such questions relevant. Will a common industrial society, giving rise to similar sociological structures, provide a sufficient framework of unity? Since there are different models of industrial society, will the differences prove to be more important than the similarities? Will differences of language, race, nationality, culture, religion, and ideology be overcome to the extent of making a measure of political unity possible? Will it become a sufficiently coherent entity to support a unitary regime?

Will the community of mankind ever become real? Or will it remain forever a vision out of the pages of Dante, a poet's dream and a publicist's slogan, having no practical relation to the world in which we live? If it becomes real, then the government that alone might be able to deal with the problems of world society could be constructed. Yet there are no guarantees that even this government would necessarily succeed. We have seen that all governments are limited and that governments, although there is no adequate substitute for them, cannot do everything by themselves. The Roman example, and similar examples in national states today, were employed earlier to show that even the best of governments cannot function if certain destructive tendencies in society are sufficiently strong. Creating a world government, therefore, is only part of the eventual solution to the problems of the emerging world society. For the rest of the solution, we must look elsewhere.

6

OUT FROM EDEN

The cause of the new difficulties encountered by governmental institutions in the twentieth century is the scientific, technical, and industrial revolution that began in Europe ages ago. Its cumulative and compounded force now has burst forth upon the rest of the world as well. Although several centuries old, its consequences have begun to be fully apparent only in recent years. Its benefits are so great that all the world aspires to a share in them; but, until recently, its harmful side effects generally were ignored.

There are several reasons why the dangers flowing from the process were not perceived as fully as they should have been. For one thing, it is only natural not to want to think about matters that are disagreeable or complex. For another, a deeply ingrained habit of thought is to assume that, in the larger concerns of the world, things will take care of themselves. This assumption was embodied in classical theories in many of the social sciences, including economics and foreign relations; it also was reflected by the failure to think about such things as the effect of human activity on our physical surroundings. It is an assumption that seemed to be confirmed by the pattern of events, for things in fact once did seem to take care of themselves. What was not fully grasped was the extent of the transformation of circumstances and relationships that would be wrought by the industrial revolution. It was a change in the *scale* of human activity, and this created a difference in kind rather than a difference in degree. It was the greatest change in human history. Its effects especially are visible in environmental matters. Not long ago natural processes still flushed out industrial pollution. Nobody had to think about it. The environment took care of itself. However, at some point in the technological-industrial revolution, the scale of human activity began to have an impact that the environment could not absorb. Now industry threatens to overwhelm nature, and pollution control has become a necessary—and burdensome—additional industrial process. The disproportion between human activity and the environment in which it operates has swung around from one side to the other: the natural environment used to take care of us; now we have to take care of it.

Not merely in questions of ecological concern, broad though these are, but in every way human activity has grown to be so far-reaching that, for the first time, it has consequences that will not disappear of their own volition. A maid no longer arrives in the morning to make up the world's bed and wash the dirty dishes. We have to do it all for ourselves. Until the point of profound industrial transformation when this became true, whatever human beings did was of no concern to anyone but themselves. Afterward it was like the situation of Captain Gulliver in the land of Lilliput. To move, or even to sneeze, without advance warning and careful planning, was to bring disaster to everyone in the vicinity. Carelessness was no longer possible.

This "Lilliput Effect" came as a great surprise. Nothing in the world's past adequately prepared us for it. We had always been unmindful of the effects produced by our collective actions—and we always had gotten away with whatever we did. The reason, although we did not realize it, was that the effects we produced were too insignificant to matter. We counted on nature to nurture and care for us even when our purposes and desires were in opposition to natural processes and designs. Pattern was perceived in the movements of the universe; but no inconsistency was seen in human conduct that ran counter to it yet at the same time relied upon the pattern to persist.

The assumption that things would take care of themselves, or else that providence would take care of them for us, came from a misinterpretation of a most profound character. From the very beginning, the human race has learned to see patterns in the workings of nature. By a false analogy, pattern was also perceived in human affairs. Modes of thought derived from the observation of natural phenomena were inappropriately applied to economic, social, and political life. It was a misuse of intellectual experience. The experience in question was basic: it had been the very making of the intellect. The human mind seems to have begun with the perception of pattern in time. Its first known manifestation apparently was the notation of natural cycles: the seasons and the phases of the moon. From the moon, which ages and dies each month and yet always comes again; from the sun, which sinks below the horizon each night and is reborn at dawn; from the vegetation, which the winter kills and the spring restores to life—from these and from others as well, the human race derived its vision of events that regularly recur in cyclical pattern: the myth of the eternal return.

The attempt to cast human affairs in similar cyclical patterns began with philosophical speculation itself; but it never has been justified, except by religious faith. Physical bodies conform to measurable natural laws, the operation of which can be confirmed by observation and predicted in advance. Human events, on the contrary, are shaped by the interplay of forces and accidents that cannot be foreseen. Yet from Aristotle, who thought he saw a regular cyclical shift in the forms of government, to Lin Piao, who claimed that the countryside again and again would conquer the city, it has been imagined that politics and government move in patterned and predictable ways. In the absence of natural forces acting to create patterns in our affairs, there is no rational validation for any of these theories.

Even with respect to nature, we are now told that we were generalizing from a single episode. Human life, it is now believed, is a one-time thing; the race will die and never come again. According to biologist Jacques Monod, the emergence of life was an incredible accident; the statistical chance of its happening was zero, and so it could not be expected to happen again. Similarly, the solar system may also be a unique aberration. A leading astrophysicist, Jesse L. Greenstein, has suggested on the

basis of recent evidence that we are not in the main-
stream of chemical and nuclear processes that are
observed in the rest of the universe. The particular
system that revolves about our sun may be the only one
of its kind. Even the universe as a whole may be a unique
and perishable entity. As Einstein once imagined, its life
may follow the path of a stone thrown in the air: upward
as long as its momentum lasts, then downward as it falls
back and collapses. According to one current scientific
view, after this "fall" all matter and all physical laws will
be annihilated as they sink into a universal "black hole,"
which will be the end of everything.

In our time physics has become almost as gloomy a
science as politics or economics. Perhaps scientists are as
wrong now as they have been in the past. In the future
people may laugh at our black holes, just as we now
laugh at the theory that frogs spontaneously generated
from the mud of the Nile. The point is, however, that we
can no longer be certain of cycles in nature, even those
we seem to see in the skies. Much less are we warranted
in casting mundane and human events in these cyclical
patterns.

The classics that reached their apogee in the eight-
eenth and nineteenth centuries saw innate harmony and
equilibrium everywhere. Therefore they took the position
that governments did not have to provide conscious
management and direction for society. In the Adam
Smith and Jeremy Bentham way of thinking, people had
only to pursue their own interests; an unseen hand would
guide the interests of the community as a whole. These
views were expressed in many contexts, including that of

political economy. According to the laws of classical economics, supply created demand and led to full employment. In actual practice, however, these laws turned out not to function. The hand was not merely unseen; it was also unfelt. Things, in fact, were not taken care of, nor did they take care of themselves. In the depression of 1931–33 it became especially clear that the free play of economic forces does not always ensure employment and prevent the collapse of business. The worldwide unemployment and misery of those years were blamed by the Left and the Right on nefarious persons and interests who supposedly disrupted the harmony of what was reputed to be a system. Maynard Keynes, who saw more keenly, exposed the nakedness of the emperor in his new clothes: there was no system, and there never had been one. In special circumstances, full employment might come about of itself, but usually it would have to be achieved by conscious planning if it were a goal that society had decided to adopt. Total supply and total demand would have to be considered, calculated, created or curbed, and coordinated on a conscious basis. Keynes argued that we would have to *govern* these matters, because nobody else was governing them for us. Our goals, if they were important, could no longer be left to the random whim of chance.

This should have been clear from the very beginning, for whenever vital problems of a public nature have been solved, it has been through government and the organization that government makes possible. When the ancestors of the race took the first step along the road to becoming human, by leaving the forest and learning to form groups in which to hunt and fight for food, it was government that made possible the success of the enterprise. It has been the same at every step along the way. The development and diffusion of technology and culture were the result of the human ability to come together and function as a group. Even the carelessness of the young, the freedom of the dissenting individual, and the personal happiness of private people are made possible only by the framework of security that groups led by governments have created.

It is true that until now the tendency has been for governments to act only sporadically. Most matters have been left ungoverned. The illusion was that these were matters that would adjust themselves of their own accord. The reality was that they often failed to do so. However, until recently their failure was not of vital importance: the survivors of the various catastrophes picked themselves up, brushed themselves off, and went on their way.

There is a strong natural tendency to believe that the human situation has remained unchanged, but this is not so. We no longer inhabit a lush primeval forest where ripe fruits plop helpfully to the ground. Life has never again been so easy as in those golden oases from which the race of man was eternally exiled. Roaming the fields and tilling the soil proved an unwelcome and uncongenial change. The responsibility for supporting, protecting, and making our own lives is burdensome to assume; people have always tried to deny it, avoid it, or evade it. That is why, until what now seems to be the last minute, the modern world has chosen to ignore each new requirement imposed by the transformation of society in the last few centuries. Governments and peoples have preferred not to think about such things. Time and again, therefore, the foreseeable has gone unforeseen.

The frequent unexpected crises that this engenders give to contemporary life its distinctive sensational quality. Michael Harrington captured the way it feels to live today in the title of his book *The Accidental Century*. It does indeed seem that what is happening is freakish, accidental, and unplanned; but then, that has always been true. In a sense, the history of all centuries has been a series of accidents. The difference is that in the machine age accidents can have fatal consequences. A pedestrian, not looking where he is going, merely bumps into you; the driver of an automobile, not looking where he is going, can kill you. The difference between the present and the past is not that people no longer think about what they are doing, for they never did; the difference is rather that now it matters.

Planning is necessary. Coordination is necessary. Responsibility is necessary. Saint-Simon perceptively criticized the Congress of Vienna on the grounds that, because each representative sought his own country's interest, nobody spoke for the general interest. The theory that the general interest will take care of itself is a form of intellectual draft dodging. It would be more accurate to say that if the public interest were well served, private interests would take care of themselves.

The Keynesian influence has been sufficiently great so that many people now accept the truth of these propositions with respect to economics; but it is only in that limited context that they have been accepted on a widespread basis. Maynard Keynes provided a theoretical framework for the consideration of the role of governments in the management of modern economies; but he also supplied the starting point for far more. In the Keynesian theory, governments must deal with the overall quantities and propensities that classical economics believed that nobody had to think about—such as the total demand in a given economic society at a given time. The energy crisis, of which everyone became aware in 1973, shocked the world into a realization that governments also must deal with all the other aggregates. Governments must learn to keep accounts of how much or how little there is of everything in order to formulate effective policy.

In a world of finite resources and of expanding demand for them, somebody must plan to deal with the pressures, dislocations, shortages, and inflations that result. Somebody must ease the transitions to make them smooth. In a world that heedlessly disrupts the balance of natural systems, somebody must arrange to close the circle once again; or else, somebody must replace the systems with others. In a world that races so quickly toward the future and is so vulnerable to destruction, somebody should look ahead and take control of the steering wheel.

The Keynesian general theory must be extended beyond economics to embrace the whole range of social phenomena. Episodes in which things just happen to work out for the best, without need of planning or coordination, should be viewed as happy, but rare, cases. The general theory of politics must envisage a multitude of combinations in which variables and constant factors meet and create situations which, for the most part, require direction and control.

The implication of such a theory is that the totality of public activity should be brought within the framework of government. This follows from what was termed the "Lilliput Effect" earlier in the chapter; some human agency must learn to become conscious of the consequences of social, economic, and technological activity, now that such activity has risen to a level where it continuously produces effects and ramifications in the world around us. Indeed, freedom can only flourish in the context of directions and limitations such as these that prevent physical disaster. The governments of the world, therefore, must expand their scope.

On a global scale, where there is no government and where functional international institutions are still in their infancy, the appropriate response to the general theory of politics is at once more complex and less satisfactory, because the institutional framework for such a response does not exist.

In international relations the equivalent of classical economics is provided by one of the traditional theories of the balance of power. It is the theory that nations should pursue their own individual interests, while an unseen hand guides the destiny of mankind as a whole. The affairs of mankind having arrived at a fairly desperate pass through lack of management, it seemed evident early in the twentieth century that some more visible hand should take charge. The leaders of various nations, of course, have proposed themselves, their countries, and their ideologies as the proper guides to the future. The universalist aspirations of nazism, of communism, and even of Wilsonian idealism have now led to a reaction. Inspired by Charles de Gaulle, the chancelleries of the world have reverted to a frankly exclusive concern with national interests. So great has been the influence of the dead French leader that foreign policies continue to be analyzed in terms of the extent to which they are Gaullist or not, even though his traditionalist conception of the balance of power could have been appropriate only to an era long since past.

De Gaulle pursued a visionary ideal. Despite its historic beauty, it was too small a vision for the world in which we now live. Like Clemenceau, he believed in France; like Clemenceau, he did not believe in humanity. It is true that he expected and understood that the leaders of other nations also would pursue their own selfishly narrow interests: he did not claim a right for his own nation that he denied to others. His admirers called it honesty; his peers called it realism; and his enemies called it cynicism. Call it what you will, it did not rise to the occasion. Other leaders might be bound by narrow nationalism, but that was no reason for de Gaulle, who was capable of a larger and longer vision, to make his mind and policy as narrow as the mind and policy of the others. For all of his grandeur and style, it limited him. He was the Achilles of our time, and this was the heel of his statecraft.

De Gaulle saw the reality of the national state; and he also saw the hypocrisy of some who claimed to speak for wider interests. Many of the multinational schemes he scorned were indeed manipulations in disguise, while others were foolishly optimistic and unreal. They assumed the existence of transnational loyalties and ignored the existence of nationalism. They were proposed by shallow men. The eighteenth-century ironist who had become president of France saw through them all. De Gaulle's strength was that he knew what was false. His weakness was that he did not know what was true.

The emerging truth of our contemporary world is that there are now vital concerns that transcend narrow national interests. A policy that opposes the preponderance of power is limited and merely negative in its objectives. It is a sterile conception offering no positive and constructive alternative to the political program that it will not permit to be carried into effect.

The modern world needs a constructive and more rounded policy of balance—that is, one that does not stop at forbidding hegemony, but goes on instead to propose a common course of action. Such a policy must take into account the relevant national views, interests, and susceptibilities that are involved, but it must also take into account the fact that there are problems of significance to the whole world that must be resolved. Achieving a stable balance of power, if it proves possible to do so, would itself constitute a valuable step on the road to creation of an orderly world. Moreover, by making it impossible for any interested party to impose its own solution, such a balance guarantees that any decisions that are reached will represent a wider point of view. Matters cannot stop there, however, at mere accommodation of rival national viewpoints and compromise of international disputes. The M.I.T. study of the limits of world economic growth, sponsored by the Club of Rome and made public in 1972, dramatized the absence of a global point of view, for the debate to which it led took place in a political vacuum. The debate certainly was relevant to the world's affairs, for at some point growth will no longer be feasible on a finite planet, and it is clearly of importance to determine that point in advance. Yet if no government is prepared to transcend its private concern with growing richer and more powerful than its neighbors in order to reach a global view that will keep the competitive growth from destroying the world, then there is no real basis for a political agency in operation to pursue a policy aimed at ensuring human survival. This is the dead end to which the mordant logic of Gaullism leads.

There is no unseen hand. To the extent that national governments find it possible to act in concert, they must undertake to guide the political, economic, and social destiny of the human race, because no other agency is doing it. Theirs is the responsibility for setting goals as well as for achieving them. Unless they take charge of the range of haphazard human activities, things will continue to happen that we cannot afford or do not want. Internationally as well as nationally, organization is required in order to bring events back under control. The challenge of our time is to transpose Kantianism from thought to action: that is, the objective is to use the human mind not merely to order and organize perception and cognition, but also to order and organize events and circumstances.

There are no givens in the situation. The pieces in the jigsaw puzzle do not necessarily fit together, and there is no assurance that we can shape them in such a way that they will do so. It may be that the type of industrial society we have today cannot last. It may be that we will run out of materials we cannot synthesize. It may be that the system cannot be made to cohere. It may be that our civilization, like Rome's, costs too much to operate. Our civilization has made individual freedom possible, but it has also increased so markedly the power of individuals to harm whole groups that society is vulnerable as never before to the crazed terrorist with his finger on the trigger. That human beings are dangerous is something we have forgotten. What is needed is the political equivalent of the handshake: a gesture of precaution transmuted into an expression of comradeship.

The lack of cohesiveness typical of our modern world puts the maximum strain on society, and this requires the maximum expense. It is difficult to accomplish public goals when the public itself is apathetic and uncooperative, and while elements of the population are estranged or hostile. Society today can afford neither crime nor punishment. The coincidence in time of a socially uncohesive society with an expansion of new activities that also require governing has caused the beginning of governmental collapse throughout the world.

Until now choices could be conceived in the absolute, one-factor terms of classical political philosophy, such as: "What is just?" Now, when the things we do create such serious problems of cost, questions must become relative and double-entry: "Is it desirable?" becomes "Is it worth

it at the price?" Traditional political thought was like a
menu without prices; it has now been outmoded by an
ecological situation in which nothing is free anymore and
a social situation in which, increasingly, you can give to
Peter only by taking from Paul. What is justice then?

The Chicago school of political scientists has made a
valuable contribution to the consideration of such issues
by suggesting that political societies be viewed in terms of
whole systems in which elements interact and are
interdependent. To the extent that it is possible to do so,
this is surely the right way to think about policies and
their consequences. If you can see all of the ramifications
that will flow from a given decision, and if you can
picture in all of its contours the situation that will result
from it, then you are in a position to judge whether or not
the decision should be made. It affords the proper basis
for comparison of policy alternatives if you can visualize
the different situations that would result from their
adoption and then apply your system of values to a
determination of which total situation would be preferable. The question is how to do it. Obviously, it can never
be done really adequately or with any certainty, for the
future and its contingencies are unknowable in advance.
Yet it is necessary to try, for all decisions should be based
on prediction; and in doing so, it is important to
recognize that reality is dynamic rather than static. The
systems approach, therefore, can enrich political dis-
course and extend its range if it is employed flexibly and
without dogmatism.

This approach is all the more valuable today to the
extent that it illuminates the available choices, for ours is

a time in which it is increasingly difficult to arrive at decisions. The choices are hard; and the people of most nations seem disinclined to face decisions involving unattractive alternatives. The modern world recoils against government, which epitomizes the need for choice. As the frontiers end and the possibilities narrow, politics centers increasingly on the priorities established in the budget. Governments break down as society refuses to accept the need for priorities, believing that one thing can be gained without giving up another. Government, which begins with the calendar, ends with the budget.

The cruel paradox of the industrializing revolution is that, while forcing society to expand the range of government and to rely on government to an ever greater extent, it at the same time shatters the social foundations necessary to enable government to survive and function. Until recently we saw only the benefits and triumphs of the industrializing process. Now we have probably swung too much the other way. We see that industrial society lowers standards and that in many ways it disrupts the fabric, quality, and stability of life. It deprives the young of a sense of values and the old of a sense of personal worth. It awakens or creates desires that cannot be satisfied and leads to intense and prevalent frustration, which, in turn, brings conflict, rage, and violence. In all of these ways and in many others besides, it tends to destroy the civic virtue and the sense of community that government needs and that it tries to create.

The social illness of industrial society was accurately diagnosed in its early stages. Comte saw that the division of labor impaired the sense of community, and he identified the "social destiny" of government in terms of holding industrial society together. *Altruism* is the word he coined to describe the desirable characteristic that had to be encouraged if cohesion were to be achieved. According to Tocqueville, the disrupting and opposite tendency was *individualism*, a term which he used to indicate a selfish and exclusive withdrawal into personal concerns and a lack of care for the interests of others or of the community as a whole. It was, as he saw it, a dangerous tendency fostered by democracy and against which democracy had to guard. Tocqueville thought that the threat to social solidarity stemmed from democracy; Comte thought that it stemmed from industrialization; Ibn Khaldun thought that it stemmed from urban life. We Americans of the twentieth century, who live in an urban, industrial democracy, reel under the combined impact of disruptive tendencies.

The full significance of the deterioration of social cohesion only becomes apparent in the light of an understanding that the purpose of government is to enable human beings to function as a group. It then can be seen that a process disruptive of the group entity is a direct negation of the governmental process; it is as death is to life. If the process of negation proves to be of sufficient force, then the institution of government is not merely weakened; it is destroyed. The socially corrosive tendencies of modern life therefore represent more than a challenge to the discharge of certain specific responsibilities by governmental institutions. They represent a challenge to everything that governments do, because they endanger the functional existence of governmental institutions and processes for all effective purposes.

If these tendencies necessarily inhere in every industrial society, and if they cannot be overcome, then we have been quite wrong about the industrial revolution. We had thought it to be one of the alternatives open to human society; but if it cannot function without destroying society, it is not an alternative at all: it is a fatal error. Its virtue, we had thought, was that it *worked;* it was the unique method of achieving the economic aspirations of mankind. If it renders society ungovernable, however, it becomes a method that is, in fact, unworkable. Moreover, its consequences may leave the world far worse off than had it never been attempted, for it continues to deplete natural resources and to destroy natural systems that previously had sustained life on the planet. Thus, it is vitally important to develop techniques that will effectively counteract the socially disintegrating tendencies of the industrial revolution—if at all possible. The difficulties are admittedly immense, for the disintegration accelerates at a dizzying pace.

Indeed, the peculiar viciousness of the process is that it snowballs. This follows from the role of government leadership in attracting individuals to form a group. The process was illustrated in chapter 3 by a passage in which Claude Levi-Strauss showed how tribes came together or fell apart as a consequence of the success or failure of group government. It is the negative part of this process that we observe at work today. The loss of social solidarity causes governments to become less effective and more expensive than they would otherwise prove to be. Governmental incompetence is in itself a cause of group disintegration; so the decline in the quality of government, which is an effect of the loss of social solidarity, itself causes a further erosion of social solidarity, which in turn drags down government yet further, causing additional crumbling of cohesion.

A major objective of the modern world must be to reverse the process. A broad governmental program to do so must make use of all the social sciences. The task of sociology is to formulate a strategy for restoring the sense of community. The task of urban and industrial planning is to restructure patterns of living and working so as to help accomplish such a strategy. The task of technology is to adopt alternatives that can accomplish the same industrial goals but without the harmful side effects. The task of international relations is to carry through a program of careful diplomacy and the creation and strengthening of functional transnational institutions, in order to prepare the way for a widening of governmental institutions to correspond with widening responsibilities. The task of political science is to improve the art and practice of government so that governments can attract loyalties and help to create a community by their competence and success.

If academic political science is not as far along the way as the other sciences, it is not merely because of the difficulties and uncertainties of the task. It is also because political science has not believed that this is its primary task. The older generation of authorities in the field essentially were satisfied with the state of industrial democratic governments in our time and with their inherent capacity to develop appropriate responses to future needs whenever such needs should arise. This attitude was made explicit in the works of such men as Charles Merriam, who was quoted and discussed at some length in chapter 1 because he was typical as well as influential in this respect, and because he articulated so clearly what everybody in his intellectual circle then thought. The present generation of political scientists tends to express itself in a different vocabulary and to think about certain kinds of issues in a different sort of way. Even the Chicago school, which derives from the teachings and writings of Merriam, has gone beyond him in a number of ways and has developed a rich variety of conceptions and techniques of its own. Yet the same underlying attitude is there, as demonstrated by the preoccupation with the development of modern regimes in other countries, when taken in conjunction with what they mean by the word *modern*. "Anglo-American politics most closely approximates the model of a modern political system," an outstanding work of the Chicago school candidly asserts. In other words, the basic assumption from which they are working is that ours is the best of existing systems, and thus the problem in world politics is to extend the benefits of our kind of government to the other peoples of the world. It is a view that is shared widely, in practical life as well as in the academic community. Since 1945 many of the leading figures in American life have concerned themselves with the question of how to extend democratic government to the areas that now fall within the Soviet orbit and also to the areas that are sometimes called the third world. The Soviet government prevented its own people and those of eastern Europe from following us; but in the economically less-developed countries, Americans saw the opportunity to carry out such a program.

Missionaries to the third world, leading figures in the United States and Europe have tried for decades to help the emerging countries develop democratic governments of their own. Governments, universities, private foundations, industrial concerns, trade union federations, and other groups have aided in the endeavor. What has happened so far is well known: military dictatorships have seized and kept power in most of these countries. Political stability is believed to be a prerequisite to economic growth, and dictatorship aims at achieving it. The examples of Kemalist Turkey and Stalinist Russia show that a sweeping modernization of society and rapid economic and industrial growth can be accomplished by authoritarian regimes of an extremely simple sort. A sophisticated government is not necessary, nor are liberal democratic values essential, in order to reach the particular goals in question. Indeed, these goals have been achieved by regimes of a quite contrary character. It is rather the sophisticated liberal governments of modern nations that have failed to achieve their objectives. The paradox is that the goals of advanced industrial societies, such as our own, have shown themselves increasingly difficult to attain in recent years; and success continues to elude us.

A comparison of the third-world experience with that of the advanced industrial nations reveals a simple but unexpected truth: it is not the less-developed nations that need modern government; it is the modern nations that need, but do not have, modern government. In this context a modern government means one that can respond adequately to the problems, needs, and opportunities of an advanced industrial society. No such government exists at the present time. None even approximates it. It is true that when compared with the Soviet Union, our democratic form of government does have some strong elements of modernity in it. A modern society rests on science and therefore requires the discovery of truth. Our liberties (of opinion, of the press, of inquiry, of criticism, and of opposition) provide the techniques for uncovering the truth. In this respect we are clearly superior to the Soviets. On the other hand, a modern government must be able to deal with the tendency of industrialization to disrupt social cohesion, and here our government has not been much of a success. In a sense the comparison to the Soviet system does not really matter: if Russia fails, it does not necessarily mean that we will succeed. Industrial society presents a challenge to all of the advanced countries; one of the problems is that they still do not know it, even though they say that they do.

The government we need, but do not have, is one that is both responsible and responsive. The responsibilities of such a government would extend to all areas of human activity. It would need to take an inventory of everything that we have, whether manpower, mineral resources, energy, or food, and it would plan ahead. It would remain constantly aware of the state of scientific and technological research; it would calculate the possible and probable effects of new inventions and discoveries; and it would adopt appropriate policies with these in view. It would have to combine the opposite virtues of centralization and decentralization; it would encourage neighborhoods and other small groups to make their own decisions in matters that affect them, within a coherent framework of overall rational planning. It would plan and work to enlarge the area in which individual decisions can be made freely without endangering the interests of society as a whole. It would provide direction and coordination, while encouraging voluntary cooperation and pursuing goals that enlarge the scope of liberty. It would be based not merely on consent, but on participation.

The means to achieve these goals are here at hand. A million generations ago the protohumans set out to find again a life of ease and abundance such as they had once known in the Eden of their forests; based on reasonable assumptions, it can be said that we are now only a lifetime away from accomplishing that objective for everyone on earth. The necessary science and technology are either here or else soon will be. Only human nature and the manner in which it is affected by industrial society stand in the way. The question now is the same as it was a million generations ago: Can we organize ourselves into an effective group through government in order to survive? The difference is that now a general theory of politics requires us to invent a government that is all-embracing in its scope.

When mankind's new situation in the universe is seen

in the doubly revealing light of the need for total government and the understanding that there is no plan in human affairs except the one we make and impose ourselves, then all the issues of political science become open to reexamination and all the questions again become open questions. They flow into the architectonic question of how to govern mankind.

The political questions are various, but to all of them the response is the same. Government is, in each case, the answer; but government itself is in question. The programs proposed to deal with the crises of the modern world are premature, for they are governmental programs and presuppose the effectiveness of governmental decisions. This is precisely what is problematical. The disruption of social cohesion by the industrial revolution strikes at the heart of the institution of government; before anything else can be done, this is the danger that must be averted. In that sense the urban crisis, the current crisis in the world economy, the environmental crisis, and the nuclear crisis are all aspects of one central crisis: the crisis of government. Its favorable resolution requires the creation of a more governable society and also of a government that is sufficiently modern so that it can contribute to the creation of such a society.

Nobody yet has seen a truly modern government, but certain of its salient characteristics can be glimpsed in advance. It will be a government that pursues a constructive program for achieving an enlargement of the structure of authority in the world, whether through regional or functional integration. In the interim it will have to be adept at the improvisation of international decision making through the means of overlapping alliances. In the domestic sphere, too, it will pursue a program of restructuring governmental institutions in order to replace obsolete political units with units more appropriate to current economic and social realities; the boundaries of cities, townships, and taxation districts will be redrawn. The scope of the activities within its purview will be expanded. Its programs will reflect an accurate analysis of the causes of social discord in industrial society and will embody measures aimed at the removal of those causes. It will be a government that is constantly aware that it came into existence because of the structural and social inadequacies of its predecessors, and that its own viability depends upon its ability to overcome both of those shortcomings.

It will recognize that total government is required because of what science has accomplished in the world; but it will know also that government by itself is not enough, and that it can endure only through the support of an adequate sense of community. Yet it will exist as a government because community by itself also is not enough; voluntary cooperation can provide the basis of political order only within the purview of governmental coordination and direction. A million generations of evolutionary history will have demonstrated to it the immense range and variety of governmental techniques; but as many years of history will have shown to it also that there are limits to government, as there are to everything else. It will function, therefore, in the knowledge that failure is possible, and with a full historical knowledge of what it is that failure might now mean.

Almost everything that an evolving mankind has become can directly or indirectly be traced to the workings of government. Every project for the future depends upon the continued efficacy of governmental processes. Yet the social disintegration of modern society, if it goes unchecked, will end by rendering these processes inoperative. This erosion of social cohesion thus calls into question the most fundamental of the unrecognized assumptions to which reference was made at the beginning of chapter 1: the assumption that *government is possible*. It is so simple an assumption that it may seem almost innocuous; but in retrospect, it now can be seen that it was the basis of all of human history. Should it prove no longer to be true, then history will have come to an end.

That is why the many ways in which governmental institutions are failing and weakening in the contemporary world add up to something more significant than a list of particular political problems. Taken together, they suggest that the future of any kind of organized society may be in doubt. They indicate that the fate of political society as a whole may be at stake. Clearly it is a matter that supersedes all others in seriousness. The question of government has become the paramount issue of our time.

NOTES

2. *a new academic discipline:* It was created by Mr. Frank Davidson at the Massachusetts Institute of Technology, and was introduced into the curriculum there in the academic year 1972–73.
2. *A recent survey: New York Times,* 14 October 1973, p. 46, reporting the results of a Gallup public opinion poll.
3. *The English word for government: Webster's New International Dictionary,* 2d ed., s.v. "govern."
3. *ethologists claim:* Desmond Morris, *The Naked Ape* (New York: McGraw Hill, 1967).
3. *Jane Goodall has observed:* Jane van Lawick-Goodall, *In the Shadow of Man* (London: Collins, 1971), pp. 109–24.
3. *"there is no recorded instance":* Austin Ranney, *Governing: A Brief Introduction to Political Science* (New York: Holt, Rinehart and Winston, 1971), p. 183.
5. *the Phoenician flotilla:* The story is recounted at length in Rhys Carpenter: *Beyond the Pillars of Heracles* (New York: Delacorte Press), pp. 70–78.
5. *"the I who writes":* W. Somerset Maugham, *Collected Short Stories,* 4 vols. (Harmondsworth, Middlesex, England: Penguin Books, 1963), 2: 7.
5. *Preface to* The Golden Bowl: Henry James, *The Art of the*

Novel, ed. Richard P. Blackmur (New York: Charles Scribner's Sons, 1934), p. 327.

5. *The study of international relations has taken the lead:* Outstanding examples include James Chace, *A World Elsewhere: The New American Foreign Policy* (New York: Charles Scribner's Sons, 1973); Adam B. Ulam, *The Rivals: America and Russia Since World War II* (New York: Viking Press, 1971); and Harrison E. Salisbury, "Image and Reality in Indochina," *Foreign Affairs* 49, no. 3 (April 1971): 381.

8. *The work was greatly praised:* Professor Carl J. Friedrich, in an authoritative article, went so far as to say that *Systematic Politics* superseded all earlier theoretical works in its field. *Encyclopaedia Britannica*, 14th ed., s.v. "government."

8. *"Government is the oldest":* Charles E. Merriam, *Systematic Politics* (Chicago: University of Chicago Press, 1945), p. 261.

9. *"The modern long-time trend":* Ibid., p. 206.

11. *a series of lectures published in 1951:* George F. Kennan, *American Diplomacy: 1900–1950* (Chicago: University of Chicago Press, 1951).

16. *Political theorists during the years of the Cold War:* A leading example is Raymond Aron, *Democracy and Totalitarianism*, trans. Valence Ionescu (London: Weidenfeld & Nicolson, 1968). In it, he divides the political regimes of the contemporary world into two categories: constitutional-pluralistic and monopolistic party regimes.

16. *a 1972 study:* " 'Two thirds of the world's 3.3 billion people suffer severe political and civil deprivations,' Freedom House reported in a comparative study released today." *International Herald Tribune*, 15 December 1972, p. 3.

16. *They perceived the dichotomy of government in a vast historical framework:* In this regard, see particularly Karl A. Wittfo-

gel, *Oriental Despotism: A Comparative Study of Total Power* (New Haven: Yale University Press, 1957). According to Wittfogel, sixteenth- and seventeenth-century European traders and travelers discovered that the civilizations of the Near East, India, and China combined institutional features, specifically oriental, that were despotic in a more comprehensive and despotic way than European despotisms. This was apparently (according to his account) the modern origin of the concept of the Oriental Despotism which Wittfogel, of course, explains on the basis of the requirements of hydraulic agriculture.

17. *diverse and important authors:* Among them are Aristotle, Montesquieu, Gibbon, Voltaire, John Stuart Mill, Hegel, Marx, Spengler, de Quincy, Lenin, and Rudyard Kipling, according to Steadman's study.

17. *"Asia" is a meaningless term:* John M. Steadman, *The Myth of Asia* (New York: Simon and Schuster, 1969). The contrary view is argued in F. S. C. Northrop, *The Meeting of East and West* (New York: Macmillan, 1946).

20. *The line of division is actually industrialization:* Yet there are also different types of industrial societies. "There are no grounds for believing that all advanced societies must be of the same type." Raymond Aron, *The Industrial Society* (New York: Frederick A. Praeger, 1967), p. 47.

20. *failure of southern governments . . . to industrialize:* "(T)he illusions of the early years of independence about rapid development have died. No developing country is now emphasizing industrialization." "Survey of Africa's Economy," *New York Times*, 4 February 1973, p. 19.

22. *The Baruch-Acheson-Lilienthal plan:* This United States proposal for the international control of atomic energy was advanced in 1946. Its full implications were discussed at that time in the first edition of the famous textbook by

Hans Morgenthau, *Politics among Nations: The Struggle for Power and Peace* (New York: Alfred A. Knopf, 1948), pp. 252–55.

22. *cheap and easily-made nuclear weapons: Observer* (London), 9 February 1969, p. 6.

23. *A currently prevailing view:* See Louis J. Halle, "Lessons of the Nuclear Age," *Encounter* 30, no. 3 (March 1968): 17.

25. *according to a widely-respected study:* John Erickson, *Soviet Military Power* (London: Royal United Service Institute for Defence Studies, 1971).

25. *some of its opponents' most persuasive arguments:* See Donald Brennan, "The Case for Missile Defense," *Foreign Affairs* 47, no. 3 (April 1969): 433.

26. *The projected military budget: New York Times*, 5 February 1974, p. 22.

27. *an authoritative study by the United States Tariff Commission: Wall Street Journal*, 13 February 1973, p. 2.

27. *These figures have been contested:* Ibid.

28. *The three hundred largest industrial corporations:* A syndicated column by Jack Anderson, incorporating these lurid projections, appeared in the *New York Post*, 3 April 1972, p. 30.

28. *fifty-one of the world's one hundred biggest money powers: Wall Street Journal*, 18 April 1973, p. 1.

28. The Wall Street Journal *suggested:* Ibid.

28. *What these unions want: Wall Street Journal*, 23 April 1973, pp. 1, 14. *Newsweek*, 20 August 1973, p. 49.

29. *there are those who propose a central bank for the modern world: New York Times*, 21 February 1973, p. 55.

29. *decisions as to how the scarce resources should be shared:* "Government and industry officials say global petroleum allocation is now mainly in the hands of the giant oil companies, in the absence of any international program

for sharing the supplies." *International Herald Tribune*, 24 December 1973, p. 2.

30. *jeopardizing children, even those unborn and those unconceived:* *Observer* (London), 6 July 1969, p. 1.

31. *Bilateral talks:* New York Times, 1 February 1973, p. 2.

31. *smothering:* International Herald Tribune, 9 August 1965, p. 1, quoting Dr. Morris Neiburger.

31. *depletion of the earth's oxygen:* Time, 10 May 1968, p. 53; Dr. Lamont C. Cole, "Can the World be Saved?" *New York Times* magazine section, 31 March 1968, p. 35.

31. *destruction of the ozone:* New York Times, 12 February 1963, p. 9; *International Herald Tribune*, 30–31 December 1972, p. 3; and 7 November 1972, p. 4.

31. *drought and famine:* New York Times, 15 March 1966, p. 19.

31. *dinosaurs:* Observer (London), 2 July 1972, p. 5.

31. *mice:* New York Post, 5 May 1971, p. 66.

32. *The curious sects:* Christopher Hill, *The World Turned Upside Down* (London: Temple Smith, 1972).

32. *Astronomers had predicted:* W. H. G. Armytage, *Yesterday's Tomorrows* (London: Routledge & Kegan Paul, 1968), p. 10.

32. *the tenth century:* Robert-Henri Bautier, *The Economic Development of Medieval Europe* (London: Thames and Hudson, 1971), p. 60; Robert S. Lopez, *The Birth of Europe* (New York: Evans, 1967), pp. 108–45.

32. *life is a one-time thing:* Jacques Monod, *Chance and Necessity*, trans. Austryn Wainhouse (New York: Alfred A. Knopf, 1971); R. F. Dasmann, *Planet in Peril?* (Harmondsworth, Middlesex, England: Penguin Books-UNESCO, 1972), p. 12.

33. *DDT:* R. F. Dasmann, pp. 18–20.

33. *the environmentalists may be wrong:* Observer (London), 13 May 1973, p. 5.

36. *Charles Merriam was able to write:* Merriam, p. 79.

37. *"all government has to do"*: Algernon Cecil, *Queen Victoria and Her Prime Ministers* (London: Eyre & Spottiswoode, 1953), p. 88.

37. The nineteenth-century growth of government . . . *has been termed a "revolution"*: Oliver MacDonagh, *A Pattern of Government Growth: 1800–1860* (London: MacGibbon & Kee, 1961), p. 320.

40. *French student rioters in 1968:* It was "a general and inclusive attack directed against the intolerable mediocrity of a consumers' society and the petty tyranny of a centralized state," according to a persuasive article by Professor Alain Silvera, "The French Revolution of May 1968," *Virginia Quarterly Review* 47, no. 3 (Summer 1971): 336–53.

42. *Uruguay:* V. S. Naipaul, "A Country Dying on its Feet," *Observer* (London), 10 February 1974, p. 25.

45. *"lost all control"*: Samuel Dill, *Roman Society in the Last Century of the Western Empire*, 2d ed. (1899; reprint ed., Cleveland: World Publishing Company, Meridian Books, 1958), p. 229.

2

46. *traces still remain of roads:* Victor W. Von Hagen, *Roman Roads* (London: Weidenfeld & Nicolson, 1967).

47. *The great growth in the municipal population of Rome led to disturbance:* Lily Ross Taylor, *Party Politics in the Age of Caesar*, Sather Classical Lectures, vol. 22 (Berkeley: University of California Press, 1949), p. 5.

47. *pervasive violence:* P. A. Brunt, "The Roman Mob," *Past and Present* 35 (Oxford: December 1966): 3.

47. *The Roman legislature was weighted:* Taylor, p. 51.

48. *Commencing in the second century B.C., Romans claimed to see the*

decay: Santo Mazzarino, *The End of the Ancient World,* trans. George Holmes (New York: Alfred A. Knopf, 1966), p. 20.

49. *As Ferdinand Lot has suggested:* Ferdinand Lot, *The End of the Ancient World and the Beginnings of the Middle Ages,* trans. Philip and Mariette Leon (New York: Harper & Row, Harper Torchbooks, 1916), p. 172.

49. *Edward Gibbon claimed to have been inspired:* It has been suggested that Gibbon's account of how this vision came to him is partly or entirely fictional. David P. Jordan, *Gibbon and His Roman Empire* (Urbana: University of Illinois Press, 1971), pp. 17–23.

50. *According to Santo Mazzarino:* Mazzarino, p. 18.

50. *As Polybius wrote:* Polybius, *Histories* 1:4:1.

51. *As Geoffrey Barraclough has written:* New York Review of Books 14, no. 11 (4 June 1970): 51.

51. *Gibbon himself:* Jordan, p. 213.

52. *even Michael Rostovtzeff:* M. Rostovtzeff, *The Social and Economic History of the Roman Empire,* 2d ed., rev. P. M. Fraser, 2 vols. (Oxford: Clarendon Press, 1957), 1: 451.

53. *In China:* Mark Elvin, *The Pattern of the Chinese Past* (London: Eyre Methuen, 1973), pp. 21–24; *Nagel's Encyclopedia-Guide China,* 3d ed., s.v. "history."

53. *in India:* Jawaharlal Nehru, *Glimpses of World History* (New York: John Day, 1942), pp. 49–52.

54. *The history of Sumer is the earliest:* For an account of the current search for the remains of pre-Sumerian civilization, see Geoffrey Bibby, *Looking for Dilmun* (New York: Alfred A. Knopf, 1969).

54. *Five thousand years ago:* Mazzarino, pp. 17–19; William H. McNeill, *The Rise of the West: A History of the Human Community* (Chicago: University of Chicago Press, 1963), pp. 41–48.

54. *These wars may have been the primary cause:* Rostovtzeff, 1:1.

54. *As Werner Jaeger wrote:* Werner Jaeger, *Paideia: the Ideals of Greek Culture,* trans. Gilbert Highet, 3 vols. (New York: Oxford University Press, 1944), 3: 288–89.

56. *Stringfellow Barr has written:* Stringfellow Barr, *Consulting the Romans* (Santa Barbara: Center for the Study of Democratic Institutions, 1967), p. 8.

56. *the way up and the way down:* The reference is to the aphorism of Heraclitus cited as Fragment 108 in the numbering system followed by Philip Wheelwright, *Heraclitus* (Princeton: Princeton University Press, 1959).

56. *A rootless army of the poor:* Proletarians and poor peasants replaced the peasantry as a whole. Rostovtzeff, 1:25.

57. *Sir Ronald Syme has described:* Ronald Syme, *The Roman Revolution* (Oxford: Clarendon Press, 1939).

57. *"The new army owed":* Rostovtzeff, 1: 25, 40.

57. *in time of war they were inadequate:* A. H. M. Jones, *The Later Roman Empire 284–602,* 3 vols. (Oxford: Basil Blackwell, 1964), 1:9.

58. *the distortions and evils that it introduced into the economy:* Rostovtzeff, 1: 15–23.

58. *a program of urbanization:* Rostovtzeff, 1:49–51.

58. *"The successes of Trajan":* Rostovtzeff, 1: 355.

59. *the real value of Roman metal coinage:* Jones, 1: 27.

59. *"It is thus plain":* Rostovtzeff, 1: 466.

59. *The very terms* inflation *and* deflation: *Everyman's Encyclopaedia,* 5th ed., s.v. "inflation."

59. *an almost unbroken rise.* R. J. Ball and Peter Doyle, eds., *Inflation: Selected Readings* (Harmondsworth, Middlesex, England: Penguin Books, 1969), p. 7. The nature and possible cure of the inflation are matters subject to controversy. Ibid. For another recent point of view, see Robert Lekachman, *Inflation: The Permanent Problem of*

Boom and Bust (New York: Random House, Vintage Books, 1973).

60. *there was a gradual relapse:* Rostovtzeff, 1: 514, 532.

60. *"They took over a heavy heritage":* Rostovtzeff, 1: 505, 513.

61. *The solution of Diocletian:* Rostovtzeff, 1: 449–50, 518–19.

61. *"A wave of resignation":* Rostovtzeff, 1: 523.

61. *"they never asked":* Rostovtzeff, 1: 532.

61. *Thucydides:* John H. Finley, Jr., *Thucydides* (Ann Arbor: University of Michigan Press, Ann Arbor Paperbacks, 1963), p. 87.

62. *Sallust and Julius Caesar:* Mazzarino, p. 27.

63. *those of the third century:* A current view is that Rostovtzeff exaggerated the effect of the civil wars of the third century in terms of the collapse of ancient society. Peter Brown, *The World of Late Antiquity from Marcus Aurelius to Mohammed* (London: Thames and Hudson, 1971).

63. *Rostovtzeff has reasoned:* Rostovtzeff, 1: 365.

63. *is echoed:* Mazzarino, for example.

64. *"the sole creative genius":* Theodor Mommsen, *The History of Rome*, 4 vols. (Everyman's Library, 1911), 4: 424.

64. *Theodor Mommsen:* Ibid., 4: 424–527.

65. *Some have suggested:* Mason Hammond, *City-State and World State in Greek and Roman Political Theory until Augustus* (Cambridge: Harvard University Press, 1951).

65. *it did think of the idea:* J. A. O. Larsen, *Representative Government in Greek and Roman History, Sather Classical Lectures*, vol. 28 (Berkeley: University of California Press, 1955); Rostovtzeff, 1: 36; Taylor, p. 55.

65. *A tale from the far ends of Eurasia:* Homer H. Dubs, *A Roman City in Ancient China* (London: China Society, 1957).

67. *probably less than 1 percent:* Graham Webster, *The Roman Imperial Army* (London: A. C. Black, 1969), p. 109.

67. *more than a military force:* Ramsay MacMullen, *Soldier and*

Civilian in the Later Roman Empire (Cambridge: Harvard University Press, 1963).

67. *"No one who reads"*: A. H. M. Jones, *The Decline of the Ancient World* (New York: Holt, Rinehart and Winston, 1966), p. 367.

70. *"To Seleucus"*: W. W. Tarn, *The Greeks in Bactria and India*, 2d ed. (Cambridge: Cambridge University Press, 1951), p. 5.

71. *Mark Elvin recently argued:* Elvin makes this a major conclusion of his book, cited above in this chapter at p. 53.

72. *"Too vast"*: Henri Berr, cited in Preface to Lot, *The End of the Ancient World* . . . , p. xxxviii, cited above at p. 48.

73. *Mitrany:* David Mitrany, *A Working Peace System* (Chicago: Quadrangle Books, 1966).

73. *Morgenthau:* Hans Morgenthau, *Politics among Nations: The Struggle for Power and Peace*, 5th ed. (New York: Alfred A. Knopf, 1973).

3

76. *"He who thus"*: Aristotle, *Politics* 1:2.

77. *institutions created for one reason:* Ibid.

78. *an agricultural revolution . . . in at least two or three different parts of the world:* William G. Solheim, II, "An Earlier Agricultural Revolution," *Scientific American* 226, no. 4 (April 1972): 4.

78. *a settling down of much of the human race:* A full appreciation of these events and of their significance has been provided in J. Bronowski, *The Ascent of Man* (Boston: Little, Brown and Company, 1973).

79. *perhaps only about eighteen years:* This is suggested by

evidence obtained in Greece and is supported by the first results of excavations at Sharh-I-Sokhta in Iran, conducted by a joint Irano-Italian team led by Dr. Marizio Tosi. "The only available large-scale study of Bronze Age demography refers to mainland Greece and suggests that the average life expectancy was about 18 years. The initial evidence at Sharh-I-Sokhta corroborates this." *Times* (London), 11 December 1972, pp. 1, 4.

80. *modern historians have only just begun to grapple:* K. Folca, trans., and Peter Burke, ed., *A New Kind of History: From the Writings of Lucien Febvre* (London: Routledge & Kegan Paul, 1973); Marc Bloch, *The Historian's Craft*, trans. Peter Putnam (Manchester: Manchester University Press, 1954).

80. *The ascent to civilization:* This paraphrases Bronowski.

80. *Indus valley civilization:* This is the most recent theory as to how it came to an end. The earlier theory was that it succumbed to Aryan conquest. But the 1964–65 expedition of the University of Pennsylvania and the Pakistani Department of Archaeology produced evidence indicating that it was flooding rather than armed conquest that ended Harappan civilization. George F. Dales, "The Decline of the Harappans," *Scientific American* 214, no. 5, (May 1966): 92.

81. *"Civilization may be either":* Ibn Khaldun, *The Muqaddimah: An Introduction to History*, trans. Franz Rosenthal, Bollingen Series XLIII, 2d ed., 3 vols. (Princeton: Princeton University Press, 1967), 1: 84–85.

81. *The medieval conception:* A. Gewirth, *Marsilius of Padua: Defender of the Peace* (New York: Columbia University Press, 1951); R. W. Carlyle and A. J. Carlyle, *A History of Medieval Political Theory in the West*, 2d ed., 6 vols. (Edinburgh: W. Blackwood and Sons, 1928–1936), 3: 41.

82. *steeped in magic:* The property that allowed one man to rule another must have been perceived as magical. Robert MacIver, *The Web of Government* (New York: Macmillan, 1947), p. 13.

82. *"In the beginning":* J. A. Spender, *The Government of Mankind* (London: Cassell, 1938), p. 30.

82. *the secular orientation of current urban studies:* This relates to studies of history as well as to those of current events. Thus Max Weber, in developing his urban sociology, considered the city in its origin to be not an altar but a marketplace. Max Weber, *The City*, trans. Martindale and Neuwirth (New York: Macmillan, Free Press, 1958). For the earliest cities, see Gideon Sjoberg, *The Preindustrial City* (New York: Macmillan, Free Press, 1960), a discussion of the social and ecological structure of the nonindustrial city on a comparative basis, which also has little to say about religion except in its structural aspect. See also *Scientific American* 213, no. 3 (September 1965), a complete issue devoted to cities as an introduction to the range of contemporary urban studies and concerns (all of them secular).

82. *"These usages":* Numa Denis Fustel de Coulanges, *The Ancient City* (Garden City, New York: Doubleday, Anchor Books, n.d.), p. 141. An introductory note states that this reprints a translation by Willard Small, published in 1873, nine years after the original publication in French of *La Cité Antique.*

83. *"Every city might be called holy":* But they may be called other things as well. Cf. the comments of Jean Gottman ("The city has always been the center of evil since ancient times. . . . To some extent, evil always congregates around the sacred location"), and Richard Lichtman ("One of the functions of the city, in history, has been to

create and channelize and release evil") in "The Corrupt and Creative City," *Center Diary* 14 (Santa Barbara: Center for the Study of Democratic Institutions) (September–October 1966), pp. 34, 36.

84. *"no two have been exactly alike":* Ranney, *Governing,* p. 183.
86. *highly sophisticated terms:* A lucid summary of the major modern theories is provided by W. J. M. Mackenzie, *Politics and Social Science* (Baltimore: Penguin Books, 1967).
86. *Lucy Mair:* Lucy Mair, *Primitive Government,* rev. ed. (Harmondsworth, Middlesex, England: Penguin Books, 1970).
86. *an inventory of governmental activities:* Carl H. Chatters and M. L. Hoover, *Inventory of Governmental Activities in the United States* (Chicago: Municipal Finance Officers' Association of the United States and Canada, 1947).
87. *A recent textbook:* Peter Wales, *The Elements of Comparative Government* (London: Butterworth, 1967), p. 5.
87. *A less neutral formulation:* Merriam, *Systematic Politics,* p. 31.
88. *Nuer:* Mair, p. 63.
88. *Turkana:* Ibid., p. 76.
88. *functional definition of government:* Ibid., p. 16.
89. *"Very deep":* Thomas Mann, *Joseph and his Brothers,* trans. H. T. Lowe-Porter (New York: Alfred A. Knopf, 1948), p. 3.
89. *"Less than a decade":* Dr. Ernest Mayr, director of the Harvard Museum of Comparative Zoology, quoted in the *New York Times,* 14 January 1967, p. 1. The new evidence—a perhaps human (or perhaps not) elbow-bone, found in Kenya—was discovered by Professor Bryan Patterson of the museum staff.
89. *"1470 Man":* A full account of the discovery and of Leakey's comments on it are to be found in the *Sunday Times* (London), 12 November 1972, p. 17.

90. *"a million generations":* New York Times, 15 January 1967, p. 5.

90. *Primates:* Morris, The Naked Ape.

90. *chimpanzees:* Goodall, In the Shadow of Man.

91. *nineteenth-century anthropology:* It was the theory of the American anthropologist Lewis Henry Morgan, and it was incorporated in the theory of Woodrow Wilson, The State, rev. ed. (Boston: Heath & Co., 1898), pp. 2–4.

92. *Levi-Strauss:* Claude Levi-Strauss, "The Social and Psychological Aspects of Chieftainship in a Primitive Tribe: The Nambikuara of Northwestern Mato Grosso," in Ronald Cohen and John Middleton, eds., *Comparative Political Systems: Studies in the Politics of Pre-Industrial Societies* (Garden City, New York: The Natural History Press, 1967), pp. 52–53.

93. *chimpanzees make tools:* Goodall, 218.

93. *the pertinent question about the marine mammals:* Economist (London), 19 May 1973, pp. 134–35.

94. *what is distinctively human:* This broader formulation might also be supported by Marshack's recently announced interpretation of engravings on a bone 135,000 to 150,000 years old as prewriting prenotation formal symbolism. International Herald Tribune, 2–3 December 1972, p. 3.

94. *structures to organize knowledge of the pattern of movements in the sky . . . Stonehenge:* Gerald S. Hawkins, in collaboration with John B. White, *Stonehenge Decoded* (Garden City, New York: Doubleday, 1965).

95. *calendar:* Agnes Kirsopp Michels, *The Calendar of the Roman Republic* (Princeton: Princeton University Press, 1967), pp. 3–5; Taylor, *Party Politics in the Age of Caesar,* pp. 78–90.

96. *freedom:* Merriam, p. 31.

96. *repression:* V. I. Lenin, *The State and Revolution* (London: George Allen & Unwin, 1919).

4

98. *social problems as well have been placed on the agenda for technological solution:* Alvin M. Weinberg, "Can Technology Replace Social Engineering?," *The University of Chicago Magazine* 59, no. 1 (October 1966): 6.

100. *He recalled that when he was a little boy:* The episode is narrated by Georg Schwarzenberger, *Power Politics,* 2d rev. ed. (New York: Frederick A. Praeger, 1951), p. 16.

101. *a major research institution:* The Brookings Institution. See Charles L. Schultze, Edward R. Fried, Alice M. Rivlin, Nancy H. Teeters, *Setting National Priorities: The 1973 Budget* (Washington, D.C.: Brookings Institution, 1972), pp. 449–55.

101. *privileges:* For a full discussion, see C. B. A. Behrens, *The Ancien Régime* (London: Thames and Hudson, 1967). A similar phenomenon can be seen in dynastic China: Owen Lattimore, *Inner Asian Frontiers of China* (Boston: Beacon Press, 1962), pp. 125–26.

103. *Bureaucracy, however, is a word with many meanings:* The word was invented by Vincent de Gournay (1712–1759), a French official, and later was popularized by Balzac. It has come to mean many things since then. A delineation and discussion of the different senses in which the term is used is provided by Martin Albrow, *Bureaucracy* (London: Pall Mall Press, 1970).

105. *the United States General Accounting Office reported:* International *Herald Tribune,* 22 August 1973, p. 2.

106. *human nature:* The classic reassertion of its political importance was Graham Wallas, *Human Nature and Politics* (London: Archibald Constable, 1908).

107. *Spinoza wrote:* Benedict de Spinoza, *The Political Works,* ed. and trans. A. G. Wernham (Oxford: Clarendon Press, 1958), p. 261.

108. *Leibniz scoffed:* Patrick Riley, ed., *The Political Writings of Leibniz* (Cambridge: Cambridge University Press, 1972), p. 183.

108. *"In studying the relations among governments":* D. George Kousoulas, *On Government and Politics,* 2d ed. (North Scituate, Mass.: Wadsworth Publishing Co., Duxbury Press, 1971), p. 213.

108. *According to Monod:* Monod, *Chance and Necessity,* p. 153.

109. *"contested but . . . incontestable":* Morgenthau, *Politics among Nations,* 5th ed., p. 129.

110. *Kemal knew that only Anatolia:* "Turkish diplomacy . . . could not have been successful without the severe limitation of territorial objectives, laid down in the National Pact and not increased thereafter. The heterogeneous Ottoman Empire could never have served as a basis for Kemal's diplomacy. This he emphasized again and again." Roderic H. Davison, "Turkish Diplomacy from Mudros to Lausanne," in Gordon A. Craig and Felix Gilbert, eds., *The Diplomats: 1919–1939* (Princeton: Princeton University Press, 1953), pp. 172, 209. See also Lord Kinross, *Ataturk: A Biography of Mustafa Kemal, Father of Modern Turkey* (New York: William Morrow, 1965), p. 81.

110. *At a meeting in 1943:* Lord Moran, *Winston Churchill: The Struggle for Survival: 1940–1965* (London: Constable, 1966), p. 85.

111. *Salisbury proposed:* Lady Gwendolyn Cecil, *Life of Robert Marquis of Salisbury,* 4 vols. (London: Hodder and Stoughton, 1921–1932), 4: 311–16.

112. *General Tire Company: Wall Street Journal,* 19 November 1973, p. 1.

114. *The Soviet Union has already started consolidating: New York Times,* 4 May 1973, p. 2.

118. *Not even they, however, have noticed:* Dasmann, *Planet in Peril?,* p. 76.

120. *opposition . . . focused:* For example, the House of Delegates of the New York Bar Association, in a resolution reported in the *New York Times*, 25 January 1973, p. 27. See also Tom Wicker, "The Fallacy of 'Getting Tough,' " *New York Times*, 20 February 1973, p. 33.

124. *It has been argued:* The argument and the cited figures are found in a column by John O'Reilly, *Wall Street Journal*, 27 March 1972, p. 1.

125. *a journalist:* Vermont Royster, *Wall Street Journal*, 1 March 1972, p. 12.

5

129. *anarchism in religious and idealistic thought:* On analysis much religious thought turns out not to be truly anarchist. It is true that in theory there would be no need for government if everybody would obey the word of God; but this presupposes that each individual can listen to God with his own ears, which is denied by the claim of priests and prophets to be God's authoritative spokesmen. When the prophet Samuel opposed the kingship, it was because he asserted the claim of prophets to rule; his program therefore was theocratic government, not the absence of government.

129. *it is a rich and varied tradition:* See April Carter, *The Political Theory of Anarchism* (London: Routledge & Kegan Paul, 1971); and James Joll, *The Anarchists* (Boston: Little, Brown, 1964).

133. *As Spinoza believed:* Spinoza, *The Political Works*, pp. 11, 261.

133. *Kropotkin:* Peter Kropotkin, *Mutual Aid: A Factor of Evolution* (New York: Alfred A. Knopf, 1925).

133. *"when the comparative animal behaviorist":* Howard R. Topoff,

"The Social Behavior of Army Ants," *Scientific American* 227, no. 5 (November 1972): 79.

134. *"Practically every behavior pattern":* Ibid.

134. *In only one special, but very important, area:* There are those who believe that there is at least one other area in which anarchism has won widespread support: the protest movements in the United States during the 1960s, many of which were inspired by theories or theorists of the New Left. In Alex Comfort, "Latterday Anarchism," *Center Magazine* 6, no. 5 (September-October 1973): 4, it is argued that anarchism is the proper name for New Left theories that oppose a strong central authority. In the text of this book, however, anarchism is used in its literal sense, in which it means opposition to *any* authority, whether or not strong or central. In this sense, the New Left theories discussed by Alex Comfort are not, strictly speaking, anarchist. On the other hand, the theory (discussed in the text) that the world can be governed through international law *is* anarchist, because it says that the world can be run not by a weak government, but rather with *no* world government at all.

138. *Sir Lewis Namier:* Quoted by A. J. P. Taylor in the *Observer* (London), 17 March 1968, p. 29.

139. *this second pattern:* It is the one described in C. H. Alexandrowicz, *An Introduction to the History of the Law of Nations in the East Indies* (London: Oxford University Press, 1967), and often thought to operate along the same lines as European international law.

141. *the semiautonomous states of China:* C. P. Fitzgerald, *The Chinese View of Their Place in the World* (London: Oxford University Press, 1964), pp. 5-7.

141. *"There was a recognition":* F. E. Smith, Earl of Birkenhead, *International Law*, ed. Ronw Moelwyn-Hughes, 6th ed. (London: J. M. Dent & Sons, 1927), p. 1.

141. *"a body of Hellenic public law":* Ibid., p. 2.

141. *"the common laws":* Ibid., p. 3.

142. *When Isadore of Seville wrote:* Percy E. Corbett, *Law and Society in the Relations of States* (New York: Harcourt, Brace, 1951), p. 6.

144. *although standard textbooks assert otherwise:* For example, J. L. Brierly, *The Law of Nations: An Introduction to the Law of Peace*, ed. Sir Humphrey Waldock, 6th ed. (Oxford: Oxford University Press, 1963), p. 1: "The Law of Nations, or International Law, may be defined as the body of rules and principles of action which are binding upon civilized states in their relations with one another." Also, L. Oppenheim, *International Law: A Treatise*, ed. H. Lauterpacht, 8th ed., 2 vols. (London: Longmans, Green and Co., 1955), 1: 4–5: "Law of Nations or International Law (*Droit des gens, Volkerrecht*) is the name for the body of customary rules which are considered legally binding by states in their intercourse with each other."

145. *"temperate and indecisive contests":* Edward Gibbon, *The Decline and Fall of the Roman Empire*, 3 vols. (New York: Random House, Modern Library, n.d.), 2: 441.

146. *Europe had been superseded:* A. J. P. Taylor, *The Struggle for Mastery in Europe: 1848–1918* (Oxford: Clarendon Press, 1954), p. xxxvi.

147. *Solzhenitsyn:* Alexander Solzhenitsyn, "Letter to the Soviet Leaders," *Sunday Times* (London), 3 March 1974, pp. 33–36.

147. *one of his fellow historians:* Guglielmo Ferrero, *The Reconstruction of Europe: Talleyrand and the Congress of Vienna: 1814–1915*, trans. Theodore R. Jaeckel (New York: Putnam, 1941).

149. *It was said that international law now applied to the whole community:* The most complete exposition of this point of

view and of the arguments supporting the proposition that international law has expanded in other ways as well is Wolfgang Friedman, *The Changing Structure of International Law* (New York: Columbia University Press, 1969).

151. *a deservedly famous essay:* It was originally published in 1940 in the *American Journal of International Law.* It now appears in Hans Morgenthau, *Politics in the Twentieth Century,* vol. 1, *The Decline of Democratic Politics* (Chicago: University of Chicago Press, 1962), p. 282.

154. *George Kennan has described:* George F. Kennan, *Realities of American Foreign Policy* (Princeton: Princeton University Press, 1954), pp. 18–19.

155. *the Nuremberg judgments: Times Literary Supplement* (London), 25 January 1974, pp. 83–84.

156f. *a distinctive diplomatic development of the fifteenth century:* Margaret Aston, *The Fifteenth Century: The Prospect of Europe* (London: Thames and Hudson, 1968), p. 114.

157. *Congress of Arras has been called:* Joycelyne Gledhill Dickinson (Mrs. J. G. Russell), *The Congress of Arras: 1435: A Study in Medieval Diplomacy* (New York: Biblo and Tannen, 1972), p. viii, citing Beaucourt, *Histoire de Charles VII.*

157. *"it should be treated":* Ibid., p. ix.

157. *the ecclesiastical aspect:* Ibid., p. 207.

158. *The term* great powers: Harold Nicolson, *The Congress of Vienna: A Study in Allied Unity: 1812–1822* (New York: Harcourt Brace Jovanovich, Harbinger Books, n.d.), pp. 81, 137.

158. *Gentz subsequently remarked:* Nicolson, p. 143.

160. *a leading proponent of the United Nations . . . has recently stated:* Richard N. Gardner, "The Hard Road to World Order," *Foreign Affairs* 52, no. 3 (April 1974): 556.

161. *546 B.C.:* Schwarzenberger, *Power Politics,* p. 215.

162. *the cost of armaments throughout the world:* Archibald S. Alexander, "The Cost of World Armaments," *Scientific American* 221, no. 4 (October 1969): 21. See also William Epstein "The Disarmament Hoax," *World Magazine* 2, no. 8 (10 April 1973): 24.

162. *"Men do not fight":* Morgenthau, *Politics among Nations*, 5th ed., p. 400.

164. *Hyde et al.:* Charles Cheney Hyde, *International Law, Chiefly as Interpreted and Applied by the United States*, 2d rev. ed., 3 vols. (Boston: Little, Brown, 1947); H. A. Smith, ed., *Great Britain and the Law of Nations: A Collection of Documents Illustrating the Views of the Government in the United Kingdom upon Matters of International Law*, 2 vols. (London: P. S. King, 1932–1935); Georg Schwarzenberger, *International Law*, vol. 1, *International Law as Applied by International Courts and Tribunals*, 3rd ed. (London: Stevens & Sons, 1957).

164. *an inspired suggestion:* Richard A. Falk, "New Approaches to the Study of International Law," *American Journal of International Law* 61, no. 2 (April 1967): 477, 480. Of course, this will bind only regimes that are genuinely constitutionalist. To achieve reciprocity it may prove necessary, as in Europe before 1914, to specify that the rules apply only among certain nations and not others.

169. *Bismarck:* " '*Qui parle Europe a tort, notion géographique: Who is Europe?*,' Bismarck noted irritably on a memorandum by Gorchakov." Martin Wight, "Western Values in International Relations," in Herbert Butterfield and Martin Wight, *Diplomatic Investigations: Essays in the Theory of International Politics* (Cambridge: Harvard University Press, 1968), pp. 89, 92, citing *Die Grosse Politik*.

169. *André Malraux recently remarked: Time*, 8 April 1974, p. 34.

6

171. *The cause of the new difficulties:* This, of course, is the question that sociology has debated ever since Comte founded it as an academic discipline. Comte, though equivocating, seemed to think that industrial society destroys cohesion, but that government can restore it. Herbert Spencer seems to have held the curious view that industrial societies naturally cohere. Emile Durkheim took the middle view: he saw social solidarity as normal for industrial societies, but also saw that there were abnormal forms of industrial society that corroded social cohesion. Durkheim's brilliance was most evident in the analysis of these forms that he considered exceptional. For a lucid and authoritative presentation and discussion of these views, see Steven Lukes, *Emile Dirkheim: His Life and Work: A Historical and Critical Study* (New York: Harper & Row, 1972), pp. 137–79. A careful summary of the current state of sociological thought in this regard, from the point of view of the London School of Economics and Political Science, is provided by Donald G. MacRae, "The Basis of Social Cohesion," in William Robson, ed., *Man and the Social Sciences* (London: George Allen & Unwin, 1972), p. 39. The leading contemporary sociologist of industrial society is surely Raymond Aron, whose works are too numerous and well known to require citation. The philosophy of the industrial revolution is less well explored; but its outlines are there to be seen in a *Muqaddimah* to the future history of the industrializing revolution—Ernest Gellner, *Thought and Change* (London: Weidenfeld and Nicolson, 1964).

174. *Lin Piao:* Martin Ebon, *Lin Piao: The Life and Writings of*

China's New Ruler (New York: Stein and Day, 1970), pp. 197–243.

174. *A leading astrophysicist:* Jesse L. Greenstein, speaking to a conference at the California Institute of Technology. *New York Post*, 21 February 1966, p. 50.

175. *According to one current scientific view:* Dr. John A. Wheeler, addressing the National Academy of Sciences. *New York Times*, 26 April 1973, p. 21.

175. *people may laugh at our black holes:* Not everybody believes them even now. Some scientists cast doubt on the existence of black holes. *Times* (London), 16 May 1973, p. 21. Others claim to have found proof of their existence. *New York Times*, 25 November 1973, p. 82.

178. *Saint-Simon:* Claude-Henri de Saint-Simon, *The Reorganization of the Human Community* (1814), in Frank E. Manuel and Fritzie P. Manuel, eds. and trans., *French Utopias* (New York: Macmillan, Free Press, 1966), p. 269.

179. *to close the circle:* The reference is to Barry Commoner, *The Closing Circle* (New York: Alfred A. Knopf, 1971).

180. *the balance of power:* Many different concepts have been referred to as *the balance of power*. According to a recent essay, the phrase has had nine distinct meanings. Martin Wight, "The Balance of Power," in Herbert Butterfield and Martin Wight, *Diplomatic Investigations: Essays in the Theory of International Politics* (Cambridge, Mass.: Harvard University Press, 1966), pp. 149, 151.

190. *"Anglo-American politics":* Gabriel A. Almond and James S. Coleman, eds., *The Politics of the Developing Areas* (Princeton: Princeton University Press, 1960), p. 533.

193. *on reasonable assumptions:* Norman Macrae, "The Future of International Business," *Economist* (London), 22 January 1972, pp. v–xxxvi: "Within the next 80 years, it is logical

to suppose that practically all of man's remaining economic problems ought to be solved. This is because even the average growth rate of just over 4½ per cent per annum in gross national products in the 1960s would enable world GNP to grow to 32 times its present level in the next 80 years—and thus give today's richest country, America, an average family income of around $250,000 a year by early in the second half of the twenty-first century, at a date when many of today's children will still be alive." (p. vi)

INDEX